Why Does My Dog . . . ?

Why Does My Dog . . . ?

John Fisher

HOWELL BOOK HOUSE

New York

A Prentice Hall Macmillan Company
15 Columbus Circle
New York, NY 10023

Library of Congress Cataloging-in-Publication Data

Fisher, John, 1947–
    Why does my dog . . . ?/John Fisher
        p.   cm.
    Originally published: London: Souvenir Press, 1991.
    Includes index.
    ISBN 0-87605-792-X
    1. Dogs—Behavior. 2. Dogs—Psychology. 3. Animal behavior
therapy. I. Title.
SF433.F473   1992
636.7′0887—dc20   92–12613   CIP

10 9 8 7 6 5 4 3 2

Printed in the United Kingdom

CONTENTS

APPENDIX

INTRODUCTION

It is 10.50 p.m. The film is just finishing and I really want to see the end of it, but the phone is ringing and I've forgotten to switch on the ansaphone. I bet someone's just been bitten, or the husband can't get into bed because the dog won't let him. Why do dogs wait for the best programmes to come on television before causing problems?

'Hello, John Fisher speaking.'

Mr Fisher, My name's Adrian Silvey and my vet gave me your name.

Not at 11 o'clock at night he didn't, I think to myself.

It's about our seven-month-old Parson Jack Russell called Zippy. He keeps trying to make love to George.

Resisting the temptation to make a comment about it not being the sort of behaviour we would expect from a Parson, I ask who George is.

George is the cat! We take Zippy to training classes, in fact he's been promoted to the next class, but we can't stop him leaping on the cat at every opportunity . . . The trouble is, I think George is beginning to like it.

It is a strange fact of life that the later the phone-calls, the sillier them seem to get. I think that most people leave it until the evening to call me because they think I do a 'proper' job during the day. I don't. This is it – amongst other things trying to allay the fears of pet owners that their dog has become a sexual deviant.

In Zippy's case it was a perfectly normal case of male dominance, combined with a tremendous surge of hormonal activity as he developed from an 'IT' into a full male dog. In the absence of another dog, Zippy was focusing his dominantly sexual urges on the poor old cat. Mr Silvey was genuinely concerned about the dog's behaviour but was reassured when I told him that one of two things would happen: either Zippy would grow out of the habit once his hormones settled, or the cat would get fed up and tell Zippy to quit, as only cats are capable of doing. If Mr Silvey felt that Zippy's behaviour was too embarrassing, or if he started to do it when the vicar called round for tea, a well-aimed squirt of water should dampen his ardour. If the family resorted to this aversive technique, they should make sure that they did not also squirt George – he had enough to put up with anyway. So did I, for that matter: the end credits were just coming up on the television screen.

I am not suggesting that I take calls like this on a daily basis. Most of my telephone conversations are about aggressive dogs, destructive dogs, howling dogs, even self-mutilating dogs – in fact a very wide variety of anti-social and unacceptable behaviours. Not many of these problems can be sorted out on the phone; they require an in-depth consultation with the family and an observation of the dog's behaviour in particular circumstances. We certainly do not lay the dog down on the couch and ask it if its mother was cruel to it.

The vast majority of the problems that a behaviourist deals with are usually just normal behaviour exhibited in the wrong place and at the wrong time. The object of this book is to explain the underlying instincts that make dogs do what they do and how we can redirect those instincts to follow a more acceptable pattern.

Owning and living with dogs should be fun. If the fun is out-balanced by misery and inconvenience, then this is the book for you.

Hold on, there's the phone again. 'What do you mean, Zippy's just bought George a bunch of flowers?'

Part One

BEHAVIOUR THERAPY FOR DOGS

1

WHAT IS A BEHAVIOURIST?

The Concise Oxford Dictionary defines behaviour therapy as *'treatment of neurotic condition by gradual training to react normally'*. To some extent, this would describe my work, but not all my canine clients' neurotic behaviour can be overcome by training. Not all my canine clients are neurotic and — contrary to the popular belief that there are no bad dogs, only bad owners — not all of my canine clients' owners are neurotic.

The causes of behaviour problems in dogs are many and varied. A more accurate description of my work would be: establishing the root causes of why dogs behave as they do; getting the owner to understand the root cause; designing a behaviour modification programme which will change the behaviour; and getting the owner to understand how to apply that programme.

Behaviour therapy for dogs is a relatively new science, but one that I believe is being accepted quicker than any other new science has ever been accepted in the past. Of course, there will always be the 'dyed-in-the-wool' element that will never accept progress — the 'I've been in dogs for over thirty years' brigade. A colleague of mine has the perfect reply to this statement: 'I've been breathing air for as long, but it does not make me a chemist.' What has caused this rapid acceptance of a new idea has been the incredible results that have been achieved in the rehabilitation of problem dog behaviour — sometimes within days.

The veterinary profession is probably in the front line when it comes to questions being fired at them about the behaviour, or misbehaviour, of their clients' dogs. Invariably, they have a waiting-room full of patients when these questions are being asked. Quite obviously they do not have the time to establish the cause and recommend a treatment programme and so, until recently, all they could do was refer the owners to the local dog training club. Teaching a dog to walk to heel will not stop it urinating and defecating in the house.

Nowadays, they have a referral avenue open to them enabling their client to discuss the problem on a one-to-one basis with somebody who has the experience, time and understanding to offer practical help.

At the beginning of 1989 I was present at a meeting between a group of people who were all working on a full-time basis with owners of pets that were exhibiting problem behaviour. Our greatest concern at the time was the advice that had been offered to some of our clients prior to their coming to see us. As a result of this meeting, the Association of Pet Behaviour Counsellors (APBC) was formed. Its main aim was to create a body of people working only on veterinary referral and therefore answerable for their actions and recommendations. In time, it is hoped that the average pet owner will become aware that such a body exists and — just as one would not have a house built by someone who was not a member of the Master Builders Federation or have one's pet operated on by a person who was not a member of the Royal College of Veterinary Surgeons — will seek advice about a dog's behaviour only from behaviourists who are registered members.

In a very short space of time, the obvious need for such an association became apparent. The APBC now has members from many different countries and in Britain alone there are over 50 clinics. Most of these are held at veterinary establishments, including three of the United Kingdom veterinary schools. Between us, we are seeing more than 2,000 canine behaviour cases per year, most of which exhibit more than one behaviour problem.

One of the benefits of belonging to the association was made plain to me only last week. I was discussing with my client the dog-aggressive behaviour of his three-year-old Staffordshire Bull Terrier bitch when I noticed that her legs were constantly quivering. When I asked if this was normal, he told me that it was but that he had thought it was peculiar to the breed; she had been doing it ever since he bought her when she was 12 months old. I asked him if she had always been aggressive to other dogs and he told me that she had, but that just recently it seemed to be getting worse. I asked him if he had noticed the tremor getting worse lately and after some consideration he thought that possibly it was.

My problem is that I keep behaving like a dog.

I know that it is not uncommon for groups of muscles to twitch in dogs at rest, especially if they have had distemper in the past; but these muscles twitched all the time, regardless of what the dog was doing. Before proceeding with the consultation, I needed to know what might cause this and whether it could be in any way linked with the aggressive behaviour. I contacted another member practice to ask if they had ever experienced a similar case. The reply was 'yes, two in fact, and both cases proved to be diet-related.'

Although there was no other evidence to show that the dog's current diet was in any way detrimental to its health or behaviour, I advised a short-term diet change and asked the owner to report results as soon as any were evident. I received a call three days later to say that the tremor had stopped completely and that there was already a marked reduction in the aggressive behaviour.

Anything that permanently affects the central nervous system will also affect the behaviour when an extra load is placed on that system. This was obviously a key factor in the aggression of this particular dog. So by pooling our knowledge and experience, members of the APBC are better equipped to offer the best advice to the client. This is only one of many examples where case histories have been discussed between us, and sound advice offered to the client as a result. Everyone benefits from this co-operation — the client, the referring vet because his or her client is happy, and each individual member because we learn from the experience of others.

I suppose the main difference between taking a behavioural approach as opposed to the traditional (training) approach, is this:

The trainer would advise a way of controlling the behaviour. The behaviourist would take away the cause of the behaviour, leaving nothing to control.

Details of APBC clinics will be found in the Appendix.

2

WHAT AFFECTS BEHAVIOUR?

DIET

We have already touched on the subject of diet as a possible causative effect on the behaviour of the dog. In the example quoted, the diet link was not clearly evident, but in most cases it is.

'You are what you eat' is a much used but often misunderstood phrase. I think we all accept by now that some of the so called junk foods our children eat might affect their behaviour and therefore their ability to concentrate and learn. These foods are a product of our changing life-style: the quicker we can eat, the quicker we can get back to earning money. The food has to be palatable, easy to store and quick to prepare. In many cases that involves flavour enhancers, preservatives and, ideally, suitability for microwave cooking.

Dog food has also undergone a major revolution and the commercial pet food industry is now a multi-billion-pound market. Gone are the days when the dog was given the family's left-overs — there is now a vast range of gourmet foods available for the pet owner to choose from. But how do we know which food is best for our dogs? If we listened to the manufacturers' claims, every food available would suit every dog. We may accept the truth of the 'you are what you eat' saying when it comes to humans, but we rarely think along the same lines when it comes to our pets. They cannot tell you that they get a headache when you give them milk – people can; they cannot tell you that choc-drops make them feel irritable and aggressive – people can; they cannot explain that a certain food sets off an allergic reaction — people would quickly link the two together. The only way that we can get this sort of information from our dogs is to be aware that 'you are what you eat' applies equally

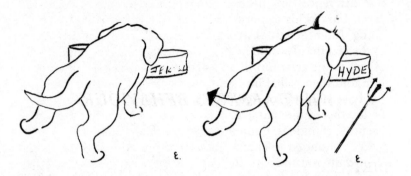

to them, and then to observe their behaviour, especially shortly after eating or drinking.

The following example illustrates what I mean. I was contacted by a very experienced breeder of Rottweilers to see whether I could offer any advice about the behaviour of one of his puppies which he had sold into an adult environment (no children, reasonably calm). The problem was that without any apparent warning the puppy, who was 12 weeks old, would suddenly start to charge around the room and become very aggressive towards anyone present. The breeder and his wife had visited the home and had witnessed the puppy's behaviour which, in their opinion, was not normal and completely out of character for the puppy that they had bred and reared. The new owners had followed all the advice that had been given and had even been presented with a video about the development of dogs — early socialisation, puppy training and other guidelines.

The breeder was convinced that there was nothing wrong with the temperament of the dog and equally convinced that the owners were not to blame. Having known the breeder for a number of years, I respected his judgement and suggested that the family should bring the dog to see me, and that the breeder and his wife should come along as well.

They arrived at the appointed time: mum, dad, granny, breeder, breeder's wife and the cutest-looking Rottweiler puppy I have seen for a long time. He was certainly a very outgoing and confident pup, but he did not exhibit any of the early signs of dominance that I had expected to see from what I had been told about his aggressive behaviour.

When called, he approached readily and happily but with

due deference (low head carriage and avoiding any eye contact). I asked his owner to call him, but I restrained him from going. After the initial struggle to go, he became quite resigned to the fact that I would not release him and he certainly did not object to the restraint in an aggressive manner. I played with him and then rolled him onto his back, holding him there for thirty seconds or so. Again, after the initial struggle to get up, he lay there quite passively. All of this told me that this was a friendly, confident, but not overly dominant puppy.

We continued to chat for a further ten minutes or so about their daily routine with the dog, during which time the puppy fell asleep at his master's feet. I was, at this stage, at a loss to explain the reported behaviour. The only evidence I had that this puppy was capable of behaving in the way everyone was telling me it could was a two-inch long gash down the forefinger of the owner's hand, which in my opinion needed stitching.

Just as I was about to admit utter defeat, the pup started to twitch his front legs – not all the time, just spasmodically, as if a fly was tickling him. Next, he woke up and started to nibble at his toes and legs. Within the space of a few minutes he was charging around my office, growling and snapping at anyone who got in his way, but what was very noticeable was the fact that a lot of the aggression was directed towards himself, in particular his legs.

I had already established that he was still being fed four times a day and that his diet had not been changed from what the breeder had recommended and had weaned him on to (the same food that had been used successfully with all his previous litters). Nevertheless, I suspected a diet involvement because frantic leg- and feet-nibbling is a classic sign of an allergic reaction. Further investigation showed that the behaviour was usually within two hours of being fed and did in fact follow the same pattern, starting with the leg-twitching.

A change of diet proved that this particular puppy, although initially able to tolerate some ingredient in the diet — now could not. Within twenty-four hours, the problem disappeared.

OUTDATED TRAINING TECHNIQUES

In the above example, the puppy was not severely punished for its behaviour, simply because it was a puppy. Had this behaviour occurred in an older dog, almost certainly a punishment-orientated training programme would have been embarked upon before expert advice was sought. Almost as certainly, the behaviour would have become worse as a result of this type of treatment. It has always been a strange human quirk when it comes to dog training, to use punishment as a training aid, and invariably we end up punishing the symptom instead of establishing and eradicating the root cause.

In view of the great strides forward that have been made in areas like education, child psychology and medicine, for example, it is sad that when you look round a large majority of dog clubs in this country, you see the same techniques being used and hear the same advice being given that you would have seen and heard decades ago. Admittedly, there are many more enlightened clubs operating and, thankfully, these are on the increase; but there are still far too many 'old school' instructors, who fervently believe that their methods work and who continue to recommend them despite the fact that, as we shall see in Chapter 3, the modern domestic dog's behaviour is being affected in such a way that training does not overcome the problems.

One of my clients recently told me that he had attended a course of training lessons with a private dog trainer because his dog was aggressive towards other dogs. At the end of the course, his dog would walk to heel, sit and lie down when told — until it saw another dog. It would then ignore all commands and attack it. When he told the trainer that his dog was still aggressive, he was told that the next time it got into a fight, he should take his dog straight home and lock it in a dark cupboard for a few hours and not feed it that day.

Even if you only had an elementary knowledge of dog training, you would realise how ridiculous this sort of long-term punishment, so far removed from the act, is in terms of having any learning effect. But this trainer makes a living by giving this kind of advice.

On the same say I was told about another trainer who demonstrated a method of stopping a dog from going upstairs. He allowed the dog up there, picked it up bodily and threw it down again. The dog hit its head on a radiator and was knocked unconscious. This same trainer proudly boasts that his methods work because nobody has to go back to him. What frightens me about people like this is that they passionately believe that they are right.

This sort of 'Micky Mouse' advice is not as rare as you would think. Undoubtedly I hear about more instances than most people: more than 55 per cent of my clients have tried the training route before seeking advice from their vet and being referred to me. There are of course some excellent trainers and dog clubs around, and my advice is to go on personal recommendation, or ask your vet to recommend somebody.

Even if the methods used are not as stupid or harsh as the two examples quoted, a lot of traditional training methods can still have an adverse effect on the behaviour that we are trying to cure. Let's take the dog-aggressive example and look at the most commonly used cure for this within a dog club environment.

The owner is told to get his dog to sit beside him and make sure that the choke chain is high up on the neck, just behind the ears. Other dogs are then paraded in front of this dog and any aggressive reaction is punished with a harsh 'NO' and a firm yank on the chain. The result is usually that the dog is frightened of showing aggression when it is in the dog club and the chain is up behind the ears — and it also learns that the presence of another dog is probably a prelude to punishment, so that when any other opportunities present themselves it is a good idea to chase off the other dog. Result: well controlled in the club, twice as aggressive outside — exactly the opposite of what was intended. (Alternative methods will be discussed in Part Three, p. 180).

Let's now look at the stupid and harsh examples of the private trainers and see what the dog might learn from their methods.

Method One

Teaching procedure	Locked in a dark cupboard and starved for a day.
Learning effect	Whenever my owner opens that cupboard door, I'm going to try and escape.

Method Two

Teaching procedure	Allow the dog to go upstairs and bodily throw it down again — preferably against a radiator.
Learning effect	Whenever that trainer is in the house,

don't go near him. If the owners develop
the same habit, don't go near them. If
they try to catch you — defend yourself
by biting.

This is what I would learn if I were a dog, because I would have
no concept of WHY they were treating me like this.

Humans have the ability to understand that the punishment
is being inflicted as a result of some earlier, unwanted action;
therefore, provided it is explained to them, the punishment will
fit the crime.

Dogs do not think logically, they learn through a series of
pleasant and unpleasant experiences which occur within two
seconds of a particular action. Considering this, we can see
why:

Using the chain behind the ears method, a dog that is doing
what it is told and sitting by the owner learns to hate other
dogs that approach it.

With method one, a dog learns to try and escape whenever
the owner goes to a particular cupboard.

With method two, a dog learns to avoid people under certain
circumstances, especially strangers who go upstairs, or
owners who try to put their arms round them.

It should be clear by now that the problem with many of the
outdated training techniques which are still widely used is: *we*
know what we are trying to teach, but does the *dog* understand?
This is the question we should be asking ourselves before we
embark upon any training programme, regardless of who is
offering the advice.

Before leaving the subject, I should like to relate an incident
that was told me some time ago. It concerned a woman who
owned a particularly boisterous but good-natured dog. She
wanted to have more control over it so she signed on at her local
dog club. On the first night, her dog dragged her into the hall
and knocked over a collapsible table which was being used to
serve tea and coffee to the assembling class. Pandemonium
broke out for a few minutes, but when it was all sorted out, both
she and her dog were locked in a cupboard for the duration of
the first lesson, as punishment. Needless to say there was no
second lesson, and although even I have to admit that this was

an extreme example, it does go to show that people who advertise as dog trainers are not necessarily what they claim to be.

ENVIRONMENTAL INFLUENCES

In Chapter 3 we shall be looking at how the way we live with
dogs today has changed dramatically over a relatively short
period of time, and how these changes can create problems with
our dogs. To a certain extent, Chapter 3 will describe changes
in the environment and their influence on the dog, but at this
stage I want you to be aware of just how *tuned in* to us our dogs
become, so that when you move on to Chapter 4 you will have
a better understanding of how these changes can affect
behaviour.

The pace of modern life is much faster and more competitive
than it ever used to be, and as a result, the number of stress-
related illnesses in humans is on the increase. There is little
doubt that our pets are used subconsciously as a sponge for the
stresses and strains of our life-style. Dogs in particular are very
sensitive to our moods and emotions, yet in spite of this they are
always pleased to greet us. It is a medically proven fact that
stroking your pet slows down your heart-beat and reduces
blood pressure. In short, dogs are good for us, even more so now
than at any time in our long association together. But are we
really good for dogs? Does this extra burden that we have inadvertently placed on the shoulders of our dogs affect their
behaviour?

There are two major areas to be examined before we can
answer this question. Firstly, whether dogs are as sensitive to
our emotions as we think, and secondly, whether there has been
a change in our attitude towards dogs.

Dogs towards us

I am sure many of us have read stories about dogs that have
acted in a manner that suggests they have a sixth sense. A lot
of these stories can be explained if you understand the other
highly developed senses that dogs have, in particular their
sense of smell, range of hearing, greater peripheral vision and
ability to spot movement. But there are still some feats that
cannot be explained away so easily. The question of whether
there are psychic dogs must remain unanswered, but this is not
the area of sensitivity that I want to explore. It is how the dog

relates to and sees its role within the family environment that is the issue here.

If we can walk into a room and sense an atmosphere of tension, can dogs?

When we sense an atmosphere, we alter our behaviour accordingly. Assuming dogs can sense the same atmosphere, how do they cope?

It is my experience that, from the dogs' point of view, they see their role within the family as much more than just that of the pet, even though that is how we might see it. The dog considers itself to be part of the unit, or pack. It categorises each member of the pack in terms of rank relevant to itself. If we were to ask a family of five humans and one dog how they viewed the rank structure, they would invariably place the dog as number six. Very rarely is this how the dog sees it. In most of the problem cases that I deal with, the dog views its role as being number two or three or, in some cases, number one.

The dog therefore definitely sees itself as an integral part of

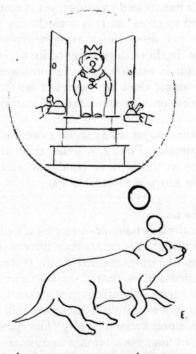

... in some cases, number one ...

the family unit – not as an addition to it, which is how we would normally see the structure. As a part of, and not in addition to, the dog is very much involved with the day-to-day family inter-actions. You only have to watch your own dog's behaviour when there is an argument to realise how concerned they become. In cases of ongoing domestic dispute, dogs have been known to act in some very bizarre ways — defecating on the bed, the table, or the clean washing. If a child started to behave in this way, we would naturally see that it was a psychological problem and a cry for some sort of help. When dogs behave in a similar fashion, we immediately view it as a training problem.

A recent case of this type involved a three-year-old male Bur-nese Mountain Dog called Guinness. He lived within an adult environment consisting of dad, mum, 21-year-old daughter, 19-year-old daughter and 18-year-old son. The family had owned Guinness since he was eight weeks old and he had been a perfect family dog. For no apparent reason, he had started attacking the 19-year-old daughter and on the last occasion had chased her up the stairs, inflicting quite deep puncture wounds to the back of her leg. Had it not been that he was perfectly bid-dable with the rest of the family, I think Guinness would have been put down.

When I saw Guinness with the family, it became blatantly obvious that there was indeed a problem between him and this particular daughter. He was perfectly relaxed with everyone else, including me, but became very tense whenever she moved or spoke. He glanced at everyone else, but watched her every move. But there was something else that was not quite right and it took some time before I was able to pin-point it. There was a distinct atmosphere between the daughter and the mother, which was noticeable in a variety of different signals. The avoidance of direct eye contact, the failure to smile at each other's replies, the distance that they kept between them — the more I looked, the more I saw.

Sometimes, my job involves me having to poke my nose into areas that I would much prefer not to poke it. Having pre-viously been assured that there was no domestic upheaval, other than the usual family squabbles, I decided to delve deeper into the sort of things that they might argue about. We all did a bit of verbal fencing for a while, until the son said, 'You're going to have to tell him, you know, because I think he's guessed something anyway.'

This comment saved us all a great deal of time. The daughter had been wanting to leave home for a number of weeks and move into a flat with her boyfriend. The mother did not like the boyfriend at all and was opposing the move — the friction between them was electric. Guinness had obviously sensed that the cause of the domestic disharmony was the daughter and he was doing what the mother would have liked to do, impose some discipline and keep her in her place.

Why the dog thought it was his job to do this is a completely different subject which will be covered in some detail in Chapter 3; for the moment, the case shows how involved the dog was with the domestic environment and how much it regarded itself as part of the family. Unfortunately, because we view dogs as different from family, many dogs are put down for behaving in this manner (and where young children are at risk, although sad, it is often the right decision). By looking at things from the dog's point of view, many of these problems are resolvable.

Us towards dogs

Many of us decide to have a dog for much the same reasons as we have done so since it became fashionable for families to have a dog solely as a pet. Recently, however, there is a growing trend to get a dog for the wrong reason.

I was recently approached by a very hard-working business couple who did not like dogs at all, wanting advice on the type of dog they should have.

Apparently their six-year-old son, who was generally looked after by other people because they were so busy, had started bed-wetting at night and become very unruly during the day. Their doctor had suggested that they get him a dog, to give him some responsibility and someone, or something, to relate to. I should have thought that the average couple might have taken the hint at this stage and decided that a parent might be able to do a better job than a dog, but they were too wrapped up in their business affairs even to consider giving more time to the child.

I refused to help and suggested, quite bluntly, that although more doctors are beginning to see the therapeutic value of dogs as pets, they should certainly not be placed into a home with people who had no rapport with them, and definitely not as a substitute for parental involvement. Needless to say, they got a dog which had to be re-homed within a few weeks because it started to become aggressive towards the couple — not the child. I know exactly how the dog felt and, although the circumstances were all very sad, I found it fascinating how quickly the dog soaked up the child's aggression towards the parents.

Obviously, the circumstances in this case were rare, but using dogs as substitutes is not. For years and years the usual pattern of dog ownership would be: get married; have children; get a dog. In recent times it has become the norm for both partners to have their own careers; equality, cost of living, material gain, are just a few reasons for this trend. The result is a noticeable change in the pattern of dog ownership: get married (maybe), get a dog, have children, get rid of the dog.

It would seem that once a couple make a commitment to share their lives together, because each one wants to retain his or her individuality and continue to pursue their own careers, having children is shelved until a later date. There seems, however, to be some Freudian need to have joint custody of a living thing, and so they get a dog. This dog becomes the baby substitute and, without doubt, those of my clients who consult me about their dog's behaviour and who do not have children, treat their dogs entirely differently from clients who do have children.

This does not necessarily make them bad owners — they would not have gone to the trouble of discussing the problem with their vet and then making the effort to come and see me if they were. Once it has been explained to them just how their involvement with the dog is the root cause of its behaviour, they make tremendous efforts to put things right and are usually more successful at doing so because there are no children around to distract them. Later on, though, along comes the baby, and then they are faced with introducing a baby into a household where the dog has hitherto been the centre of attention (instead of the other way round). The new parents are obviously very aware of the media hype about dangerous dogs, from papers which have spotted the newsworthy value of savaged children. They become understandably concerned and tension within the household is increased. Every sideways glance from the dog is misinterpreted and the dog becomes a focus for arguments.

A human psychologist would probably explain that many of these arguments are caused by a feeling of loss of freedom, by the resentment at having to give up or interrupt a career, by the strain of being a new parent, by post natal depression, and other stresses of that ilk. Whatever the underlying reason, the dog usually gets it in the neck. Even if the dog is suspected of having evil intentions towards the baby when it is first brought home and manages to stay within the family over this period, it rarely survives the stage when the baby starts to crawl, and is generally re-homed, but interestingly, rarely euthanased. Perhaps this would indicate a sense of guilt that the dog was not regarded as being as dangerous as the reasons for getting rid of it would suggest.

This sequence of events is definitely on the increase and certainly not because people plan it that way. It is happening purely because our environment and way of life are changing and, as a result, our dogs are being affected.

I was recently consulted by a retired man and his wife about their dog's habit of running away whenever they let it off the lead. The dog was a two-year-old rescue Beagle bitch which had been obtained by the wife for her husband when he retired, and she had spent a long time looking for just the right dog.

She wanted one that didn't leave too many hairs about, was relatively quiet in the house, was not too big and was already house-trained. Neither of them had owned a dog before, or any other kind of pet for that matter, therefore she had wanted a bitch because she had heard that they were easier than dogs.

I am always suspicious of people's motives when they do not become a dog owner until so late in life. I appreciate that some working couples would like to own a dog earlier, but take the decision not to because they would not have the time to look after it properly. Invariably these people have had dogs in the past, and usually, they decide to own a cat until they can spare the time to have a dog. In other words, they clearly have a predisposition towards living with animals.

The two questions uppermost in my mind were: why decide to have a pet for the first time so late in life? And why didn't the husband have a say in the choosing? The answer was simple. He had decided that when he retired he was going to buy himself some walking boots and take himself off for long walks in the country. Both of them were concerned that, in this day and age, elderly men seen walking about on their own are regarded with suspicion, especially by young girls. If he was seen to be walking his dog it would allay people's fears. This might sound strange to some of you, but in fact there was a great deal of sense in their thinking. Ask any young girl or woman how they feel about meeting a man who is out walking on his own, and whether they feel relieved when they see he is walking a dog.

This man did not *really* want a dog, although both he and his wife were now obviously fond of her — he wanted an excuse. He was prepared to let his wife do the choosing and she did so from a housewife's practical point of view. Had he decided to take up any other hobby, like golf or gardening, they would never have considered owning a dog. Because there was no natural rapport, no effort was put into formal or practical training — he automatically expected her to do as she was told because she was an adult. In fact, she probably would have done, if she had sensed some kind of bond between them. Regardless of the lack of proper recall training, no dog is going to return voluntarily to someone who subconsciously relates to the dog in the same way as he relates to his walking boots and stick. They expected me to cure the problem, much as they would have expected a cobbler to mend his boots.

Any professional animal trainer, or a trainer of human skills, will tell you that if there is no natural rapport with your subject, then you are wasting your time. All forms of intelligent life are mentally sensitive — usually between themselves — but in the case of man and dog there is a highly developed unseen emotional link. There is no way that you can mask or disguise your emotions towards your dog, the affinity has to be natural.

Contrary to how this must read, these were not heartless people. They, and especially the dog, were victims of the environment in which we live. Their decision to get a dog was made from a purely practical stand-point and not from a genuine desire to have a dog. Similarly, I am seeing more and more problem dogs whose owners obtained them as a deterrent against burglars, muggers and rapists. The question should always be asked of oneself, if I did not have a dog to guard/protect/ deter, would I have a dog? If the soul-searching reply is no, then the problems encountered will be insurmountable.

In all these cases, I advise owners on how to overcome the problem as if the relationship was genuine, but I also subtly point out that since the underlying cause is that the dog was obtained for the wrong reason, then the prognosis is not good.

The modern approach to life is that you get everything you want as early as possible and then spend the rest of your life paying for it. In the old days you bought what you could afford and saved for the things you wanted. This is a statement of fact, not a comment or criticism about which way round it should be. The pressure that is placed upon us through the 'live now, pay later' approach has all sorts of knock-on side-effects. Because we are all so wrapped up in our own private ambitions, worries and quests for bigger and better material gains, we are not communicating with each other as much as we used to do. Sitting in a traffic jam, it is hard to spot the yuppie from the brickie by looking at the car that each is driving. Everyone is pretending to be successful and affluent and the only way that others can see through the charade is if they strike up a conversation.

Within this scenario, there are two more elements that have dictated the changing face of the man/dog relationship and created yet another environmental influence: the need to appear affluent and the basic fact that, although we might be frightened of doing so, we still need to communicate with each other.

It has become evident that more and more people are buying dogs that reflect their character or life-style. Pet ownership of pedigree dogs has increased dramatically against pet ownership of mongrels. In a lot of cases, people (again subconsciously) use their dog as a funnel through which they can communicate with others. Sit on the Tube on your own and nobody speaks; sit on the Tube with a dog and a lot of people will first speak to the dog and then to you. A conversation will be struck up quicker if you own one of the rarer and more expensive breeds because people will want to know whether they have guessed correctly what it is. Owning something like a Borzoi or Saluki also acts as a statement of affluence. (Before I alienate all Borzoi and Saluki owners, I agree that the majority of them own these dogs because they genuinely like the breed.)

Keeping dogs within a domestic environment, when they have been bred for generations to perform a specific task, can create problems. A classic example would be the rising popularity of the Border Collie — probably the finest herding dog in the world and an out-and-out workaholic. Put it into a pet environment with little or no mental stimulation and it will start to herd and, quite often, nip the family members. It is then classified as a problem or aggressive dog but rarely is it either, it is just a dog with an accelerated instinct which is not being satisfied. Trying to suppress it is a complete waste of time, the problem is genetic. Keeping a dog like this in a high-rise flat with little or no exercise is guaranteed to create problems.

Using the dog as a medium through which to satisfy our needs to communicate with each other; having dogs to reflect our status; keeping dogs to protect us; and owning dogs for all the wrong reasons, are just some of the new environmental pressures being put on a relationship that has been successful for countless generations.

I think, without doubt, the answer to the question posed earlier, about whether the extra burden that we place on our dogs nowadays affects their behaviour, is yes. The changes that have occurred so swiftly are probably the main reason why there is a need for pet behaviour therapists today. Sadly for the dog, this need is going to increase as our life-style continues to change.

3

THE MODERN DOG

The changes in WHY we own dogs, although definitely increasing, still only affect a relatively minor section of the dog-owning population — most people still own dogs because they genuinely want to. Nevertheless, they are changes which affect the behaviour of the dog. By far the biggest influence on behaviour, however, is HOW we live with dogs today.

Over the past two or three decades, our everyday style of living has altered in a way that has affected our dogs — almost as drastically as the industrial revolution affected us. As mentioned in the last chapter, dogs living within a family environment see themselves as part of that family's pecking order or rank structure. Up until very recently, this has not created a problem because our living standards were such that the dog had to be considered last — not because it was any the less loved, simply because of financial and practical reasons. Today, however, we are much more affluent and enjoy an entirely different standard of living. This also benefits the dog in terms of what we allow it now, that wouldn't have been allowed before. These extra privileges that we inadvertently grant to our dogs tell them, on an instinctive level, that they hold a higher position in our rank structure than the one we think they hold. In human terms, the higher ranking you are, the more responsibility you carry and the more decisions you have to make. The same is true of dogs.

If we just look at one area of change that we now accept as standard, and consider for a moment life from the dogs' point of view, we shall be able to see why their behaviour is being affected.

As pack animals, their instincts dictate that those that sleep on the fringes of the pack, and whose freedom of movement around the den site is restricted by the others, are the lower ranking. These are the instincts of a wolf, the species from which our dogs are descended, and still govern their behaviour. Twenty to thirty years ago, people did not have central heating as a standard household fitting, they heated each room individually. As a result, doors were kept closed to conserve the heat in the rooms being occupied, which automatically restricted and controlled a dog's movements within our dens. We didn't do it consciously, it happened out of necessity.

Because our houses (or dens) were partitioned into smaller rooms to make them easier to heat, we invariably had a room that we regarded as the best room. This would contain the best furniture and would be used only on special occasions. Because we were not as affluent, did not buy on credit at the rate we do today, and had a greater appreciation of the value of what we had managed to obtain, the things in this particular room were meant to last a long time. If we were only allowed in at certain times, the dog would not be allowed in at all.

The traditional place for the dog to sleep would be in the kitchen — in fact, because of the 'keep doors shut' routine, the kitchen and the garden were where it would spend the greater part of the day. During the evening, it would be allowed to join the family in another room, but then returned to the kitchen to sleep at night. Today, the kitchen is still probably where the majority of dog owners place the dog's bed, but it rarely uses it.

Now that most houses are centrally heated and, as a direct result, we now favour an open-plan style of living, the dog has unrestricted freedom of movement around the den. It is able to occupy all the key areas that instinctively promote its rank: the top of the stairs, enabling it to view its pack from a high vantage point; the open doorways, and in particular the main entrance, enabling it to restrict our freedom of movement and guard the entrance to the den; our bedrooms, beds and chairs, the human resting places, when in fact its own super-dooper bean bag which we bought for it is left untouched in the kitchen as a visual sign of rank — I sleep where I want, but no one sleeps in my place. We do not even mind as much that the dog climbs on the furniture, for we can afford to replace it quicker than we could in the past.

These comments are not meant to imply a preference for 'the good old days', they are simply a statement of fact. We do live in a more prosperous, open-plan environment and consequently, without meaning to do so, we promote our dogs. It is little wonder that many dogs decide who will and who will not be allowed access to our dens, it's their job to do so — we told them so.

Before the popularity of commercial pet foods, as I mentioned in the previous chapter, the dog used to be given the family's left-overs with perhaps a few butcher's scraps mixed in. With what we know now about the nutritional requirements of dogs, this was probably a very poorly balanced diet. The point is, though, because we were feeding left-overs, the family would have to eat first in order for there to be any. Again without intending to do so, we demoted the dog. In a wolf pack, the highest ranks eat first and so get the richest pickings, thus ensuring the survival of the fittest.

Today, most owners tend to feed their dogs first for a variety of reasons. It means that they can sit down and enjoy their meals without having to think about feeding the dog at a time when they want to relax. They think that if the dog has been fed, it is less likely to beg from the table or sit there drooling when the family is eating. Even when they find out that it does not stop their dog from doing so, they continue to feed it first. With the range of convenience foods available, feeding the dog does not take long. However, it is not something that they want to have to do when their favourite soap starts and the evening's programme of viewing has been planned. Yet another radical change in our life-style.

There are many other areas where the modern way of life affects the behaviour of our dogs. We have already discussed the fact that the ownership of pedigree dogs has increased; again, greater affluence has had its part to play in this. Many of these dogs have been bred for their specific working abilities, and these abilities need stimulating; if they are not, the dog is going to follow its instincts and big problems can arise as a result.

Not so many years ago, mum would walk the children to school and naturally the dog would be put on a lead and go with them (usually the dog would be a mongrel). Dogs like this had regular stimulative exercise where they met children, adults and other dogs. They were tied up outside shops and passers-by would pat them on the head and talk to them. We were not so obsessed in those days with the long drawn out vaccination programmes that we have today, therefore the dog was taken out and about at a much earlier age than it is now. Research

has shown that early socialisation is paramount if the dog is going to grow up to be a well-balanced, confident adult.

Today the children are driven to school in the family's second car and the dog is isolated in the back behind a dog guard. The shopping is done at the supermarket and invariably the dog is left in the car in a multi-storey car park. Exercise is often limited to small, specially set aside areas for dogs, which are provided only so that the dog can perform its natural bodily functions. As soon as it does, it is caught, put back in the car and taken home because mum has a coffee morning to arrange or some other pressing engagement.

We have a situation, therefore, where the dogs that we own are more likely to have been bred because of their highly developed working ability. They do not receive the same stimulative on-leash walks, nor do they get the same off-leash, off-territory, activity and exercise. They live in a completely different environment from the one that generations of their forefathers lived in, and within this environment they are promoted to a higher rank through the privileges that we grant them. (See also Part Three, p. 174, Rank Reversal.)

Added to all these tremendous changes, the modern dog owner now has to cope with a rising tide of anti-dog feeling. We are in danger of getting to a point where, if the dog barks at someone, it will be accused of being aggressive. So far this year I have had to assess for legal proceedings the character, temperament and behaviour of more dogs than in all the preceding years added together. This sort of pressure makes owners more reluctant to exercise their dogs in busy areas, or even exercise their dogs at all, especially if they have a large garden to let them loose in. Without regular, practical socialisation the problems that owners are trying to avoid will be increased. If the dog suddenly finds itself in an unfamiliar situation, it will lack the confidence to cope. Most bite cases result from a lack of confidence in the dog and we should all be aware of one thing — all dogs can bite.

4

ESTABLISHING CAUSES

All the factors discussed in the preceding chapters, and many others, have to be taken into consideration before a behaviour modification programme can be advised. The behaviour therapist must take a holistic approach to the problem — in other words, every aspect of the dog's previous history and daily routine should be examined, from what he eats to where he sleeps and everything in between. If this is not done, we run the risk of missing the one vital clue that will point to the reason for the behaviour, no matter how inconsequential it may seem at the time.

To give you some idea of the investigative process, we need to know details like the following:

At what age was the puppy taken from the litter?
Seven weeks is the ideal age; earlier than this and they have missed out on learning to be a dog and may become too attached to humans. For each week after about nine weeks, they miss out on learning to be a dog within a domestic environment and become too attached to other dogs.

At what age was the dog first socialised outside the home environment?
The current practice of keeping dogs away from other dogs and public places until their vaccination programme has been completed, although important to the health of the dog, will definitely affect its future confidence and ability to cope with stressful situations if the isolation is prolonged. There is a vaccination programme available that allows puppies to be socialised at twelve weeks. From twelve to eighteen weeks is the best time to introduce a puppy (under controlled conditions) to other dogs both little and large; to children, to other adults; in fact, to as many different situations as possible.

Providing everything is made a pleasurable experience to the pup, the risk of experiencing behaviour problems later in life is virtually eliminated. For every week that goes by after this eighteen-week period, introducing the youngster to life outside the security of the home becomes more and more difficult and means that he will never reach his full genetic potential in terms of confidence and character. There is just no substitute for early experience.

Finding out about these critical early periods can help us to understand a lot about the dog. The cause of fearfulness, aggression anxiety and an awful lot of control problems can often be traced back to these first few weeks. Although nothing can be done to replace what has been lost, understanding the root cause can help us to cope and improve the problem in the future.

Details of the diet history to date
Whenever a behaviour problem arises shortly after a diet change , then the link between the two is easily recognised. However, just because a dog has been given the same food for a long period of time, with no apparent side-effects, does not necessarily mean that the diet is not to blame. In some cases, the body's defence mechanism might have been coping with whatever allergen is present, but at some point these defences are going to break down and problems will arise as a result. There are certain clues which will help us to ascertain whether diet is having a contributory effect on the dog's behaviour. Frantic leg and feet nibbling has already been mentioned, and quite often the dog will also scratch its ears, or rub its eyes and nose with its feet or on the carpet. Scratching of the chest and abdomen or chewing at the root of the tail can also be signs of an allergic reaction. Of course, there are other reasons why the dog does this, but if the scratching occurs at predictable times of the day, then the diet must be suspected.

Other signs to look for would be:

Is the dog in poor health or constantly suffering from allergies to grass or fleas?
Does it suffer from flatulence?
Are the motions inconsistent in quality, sometimes loose, sometimes firm?
On a daily basis, does it pass a lot of large, smelly motions in relation to the amount of food fed?

Does it eat greedily but never appear to put on weight?
Is the activity level unacceptable either way, hyperactive or sluggish?
Does the dog drink an awful lot of water?
Is the hair and skin quality good or is there constant hair loss?
Is it regularly eating grass, twigs, tissues, its own excreta or that of other dogs?

Each of these activities could indicate some other problem, but if two or three of them are present, then it is sensible to try a little bit of diet therapy, on which your vet will be able to advise you.

What is the daily routine of the dog/family?
It is important to establish things like exercise and feeding routines — who exercises and who feeds; what time of day the dog eats and what time the family eat; where the dog's favourite resting places are in the house, other than its own bed. Its attitude to visitors and also to the family should be noted. Does it rush forward to greet people first thing in the morning, or does it stay on its bed to be greeted by the family? How does it greet each individual when they return from work or school? All this information will indicate how the dog views its role within the family hierarchy. It often comes as some surprise to families, when answering questions about individual greeting rituals, to realise that the dog greets different members in different ways — something that they had never considered.

The family consultation about the dog is one of the most useful tools that the behaviourist has. In most cases it is the first time that the whole family has ever sat down and discussed their dog as part of their unit. The information obtained can prove to be very revealing and definitely helps everyone to understand the dog much better. Understanding is the first step on the ladder towards improving.

The answers that one receives when examining each of these areas will inevitably lead one to ask questions about other things. As the session progresses, a picture starts to build.

How does the dog behave?
Throughout the consultation, personal observations can be made about the dog's behaviour, which in itself can tell a story.

Although it is not possible to categorise behaviour problems, the way in which the dog behaves during the consultation can help the therapist to understand whether the problem is related to over-attachment or over-dominance.

Dogs that are over-attached would generally exhibit problems when left alone, like destructiveness, house-soiling, howling and barking, digging at doorways or windows in an attempt to escape and, in severe cases, self-mutilation. At home these dogs usually follow their owners from room to room, even to the point of trying to get into the lavatory with them. They are often allowed to sleep in the bedroom, basically because they kick up too much fuss if they are shut out. Once everyone is settled down in my office, I invite the owners to let their dog off the leash. This type of dog, after initially investigating all the doggy smells around, will settle down quite calmly at the feet of the owner.

Dogs that are over-dominant generally exhibit problems like territorial aggression, pulling on the lead, running off, jumping up at people, especially visitors, and a general lack of control, often described to me as hyperactivity. At home these dogs are usually granted all the privileges that denote rank, which were described in the previous chapter. When let off the leash in my office they pace backwards and forwards — usually between me and the client. They scratch at the door, they raid my wastepaper basket, they try to jump on the furniture and they bark at every little sound outside. If they do settle down at all, it is never alongside the owner. They will either lie in the middle of the floor directly between us, or take up a position by the door.

The replies that are received to the questions asked should confirm the visual diagnosis.

Details of formal training history to date
As previously mentioned, prior to seeing me, many of my clients have undertaken some sort of training programme to eradicate the problem. Quite often, rather than curing the problem, the methods employed have compounded it. I have already quoted some examples where, although we knew what we were trying to teach the dog, the dog itself was learning something entirely different. The following story should show how important it is to establish just what steps have been taken so far to overcome the problem.

Lucy was a three-year-old crossbred rescue bitch. When the

owner obtained her she was in a pitifully thin and sickly state, having been taken off the previous owners by the RSPCA. The problem was that, having now been restored to full weight and health, the new owner was limited in the places that she could take Lucy because she was frightened stiff of getting into cars, or of going through strange doorways. Lucy started to panic as soon as any move was made towards a car or a doorway and, when the problem first arose, the owner had tried to pick her up to put her in the car, which resulted in Lucy panicking and biting her quite badly.

Luckily, the owner lived locally, so she was able to walk Lucy round to my premises for me to see her. I witnessed her strange, almost phobic fear, first of all in my car park when she passed my car, and next as we approached the entrance to my office. She would throw herself flat on the floor and struggle furiously to get away. After the first attempt to get her into a car had failed, the owner had tried to coax her. Whenever Lucy started to show fear, her owner would crouch down beside her and try to reassure her. When this failed, she sought the advice of a local trainer who told her to ignore Lucy and just drag her towards cars or doors — this was in fact how she got her past my car and into my office. Once inside, Lucy was perfectly normal and friendly.

In answer to my inquiry about how she managed to collect her in the first place, the owner just assumed that she was too ill to care.

Both the gently reassuring and the firm approach had failed for the following reasons. By reassuring Lucy, she was in fact praising her behaviour. Lucy did not want to get into the car, so she refused. The owner stroked her and whispered sweet nothings in her ear, effectively praising the exact opposite of what she wanted her to do.

The firm approach was compounding her fear because Lucy was always walked on a short lead and thin choke chain and any tightening of the choker caused pain. Lucy was a very touch-sensitive dog who had hardly had any exercise at all with the previous owner. Her present owner used a choke chain because she had done so with all her dogs and thought that this was what dogs should be walked on. The constant tightening of a choke chain will eventually cause muscle and tissue damage to the neck of a dog that pulls a lot, resulting in a desensitised pain barrier. In most dogs this happens over a period of many months and is something that we don't even notice happening. Consequently, although any pressure applied to the neck by the chain might initially prove to be effective, after prolonged use the same pressure is not even felt. Lucy had hardly had anything around her neck in the past, but because she walked quite nicely on the lead the choke chain did not cause her any discomfort, except when she approached a car or a doorway — then it hurt like hell!

A situation had arisen in which first she had been praised for not approaching a car and then she had learnt that approaching a car was a prelude to pain.

We started to overcome the problem in five minutes. First we fitted her with a broad leather buckle collar and, instead of the short restrictive lead, we used an extending lead, giving Lucy over twenty feet of extra freedom. When we approached the back of my car, Lucy backed away about four feet and stood still. Obviously, the only reason she had thrown herself on the floor previously was because she could not back away farther than the end of the lead. By allowing her to do so, she was not in a state of panic and the collar meant that she was not in pain.

We both completely ignored Lucy — we did not even look at her. We both sat on the open tailgate and chatted. After about a minute, I told her to call Lucy to her and she came immediately. She got lots of fuss from both of us and we walked away from the car without attempting to get her into it — the first stage was to achieve a panic-free, pain-free approach. We went back to my office and as we approached the doorway, Lucy again backed off about four feet. We walked straight in, calling her as we went, and she followed us in without any further hesitation.

We had established the fact that the root of the problem was related to critical distance. Lucy, for some reason that we would probably never know, was wary of approaching cars and doorways (she was not frightened of traffic). She needed space and time to overcome this reluctance — much as we do when we attempt to do anything that we are not 100 per cent confident about. Jumping into a swimming pool is a classic example if you are not a good swimmer — the last thing you need is some idiot to push you. By ignoring her, we were not rewarding the wrong behaviour; by not forcing her, we were not pushing her into a state of panic; by getting rid of the choke chain, we were not causing any pain-associated aversion.

During our conversation, I found out that Lucy would sell her soul for a piece of cheese. We went back to the car, sat on the tailgate and called her to us. She came straight away and got a piece of cheese, I offered her another piece and as she was about to take it, I threw it in the back of the car. Lucy jumped straight in, ate the cheese and jumped out again — her tail was wagging like mad. We took her for a little walk and when we returned we went straight towards the car. Lucy stood back a little bit but did not back away as she had done before. I opened the tailgate and saw a moment's hesitation on Lucy's face. I showed her some cheese and threw it in the back, Lucy jumped in virtually before the cheese had landed. All that was needed from then on was to build Lucy's confidence, and it was a happy owner that I was able to drive back home.

Contrary to popular belief, using food is not restoring to bribery. First of all the dog has to perform the required movement to get it, and if it is a food that the dog particularly likes, it increases the reward that the dog receives. If using food in this way is bribery, then so is getting wages for a week's work.

Whenever we consider the problem behaviour of a dog we must first establish the root cause and take into account all other areas which might also be having an adverse effect. We then need to remove all the negative aspects and devise methods of positively rewarding the right behaviour. In other words, we need to do exactly what *The Concise Oxford Dictionary* says a behaviour therapist should be doing (see Chapter 1). Sometimes, by just removing the negative we automatically achieve the positive.

The preceding pages were only meant to give you an insight into the work of a behaviourist. In Part Two you will see just how vast and, as yet, relatively untapped an area it is for the pet owner to take advantage of.

Part Two

WHAT IS A DOG?

5

A DOG IS A DOG IS A WOLF

The answer to 'why does my dog . . . ?' is usually very easily answered — 'because it's a dog.' Much of what we regard as problem behaviour is quite often, as I explained in the Introduction, just normal dog behaviour exhibited in the wrong place and at the wrong time.

My dog has just bitten somebody! Well, dogs bite, don't they?

My dog barks constantly! Well, dogs bark, don't they?

My dog growls at me if I go near his food! Well, dogs growl, don't they? They also guard food.

All these behaviours, although totally unacceptable, are the things dogs do. If you persist in being aggressive towards your dog, the chances are that at some point it will become annoyed enough to bite you. What else can it do — send you a solicitor's letter?

Before we start to take a look at some of the problems owners encounter, we should first of all take a long, hard look at the creature we are discussing. As mentioned previously, the dog is directly descended from the wolf. During a recent investigation it was found that of ninety different behaviour patterns exhibited by the domestic dog, all but nineteen were present in the wolf. (Thousands of years of domestication have probably created some patterns in the dog that the wolf in the wild does not need for survival.)

Considering the fact that there are seventy-one similarities in their behaviour, it will be much easier to look at the wolf — an animal totally unaffected by domestication — to get a better understanding of the dog. What the wolf does naturally, we can easily accept. When the dog behaves in the same way, we think it has a behaviour problem. In most cases, the dog hasn't got a

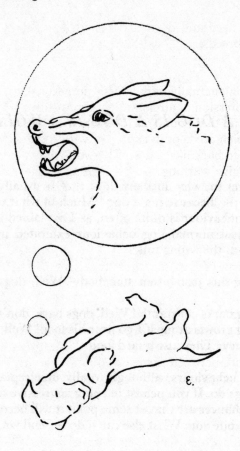

ε.

problem at all, it's just being a dog; we've got the problem of how to stop it being a dog at the wrong time.

A TO Z OF WOLF/DOG BEHAVIOUR

Whilst you are reading the following pages, remember: THINK DOG.

A.   Attack

As predators and part of a hunting unit, each member has a job to do when it comes to obtaining their major food supply of fresh meat. Some of the pack will stalk, some will turn the prey towards those that will lead the attack. These various specific behaviours have been used to create dogs that hunt and point, dogs that herd and dogs that belong to some of the fearless guarding breeds.

B. Bark

Wolves don't actually bark like the domestic dog, they let out a stupid expression of air sounding almost like an 'oofff' (if you can imagine that sound). However, it has been noticed that wolves which are kept in captivity, within the vicinity of dogs, can learn to bark like a dog. The wolf equivalent of a bark is meant to give warning of approaching danger; it is a way of summoning the help of the rest of the pack. When the pack responds, the leaders decide what to do and the rest of the pack will obey them. It follows, therefore, that the more vocal the wolf, the lower ranking it is. Higher ranks do not always need the support.

This is true of dogs, too: those that bark at you a lot are rarely dangerous; those that silently stand their ground might well be.

C. Chase

Chasing is obviously part of the hunting ritual and the learning process starts when wolves are just young cubs. They play chase games between themselves with twigs and sticks as the trophy. Good chasers will end up doing the job of the prey turners, whilst those that wait patiently to ambush the cub with the stick will probably be attackers. Watching a litter of cubs at play, or puppy dogs for that matter, you will see being practised all the skills which will be necessary for their survival later. Games that are played by baby wolves and dogs are not played for recreational purposes, they are part of a learning process. The criterion is — if it moves quickly, chase it.

D. Dig

Wolves dig! They dig dens in which to raise their young; they dig cooling holes in hot weather; they dig shelter holes in cold weather; they dig holes in which to bury food that they cannot eat at the time; they dig holes to reclaim their food; they dig up roots for extra fibre; they dig holes to investigate the movement of small creatures just under the surface — in fact, they are digging animals. As with the chasing, herding, attacking instincts, some dig better than others. From these, we have our terrier dogs — dogs with highly developed survival instincts which will defend themselves to the death.

E.   Eat

It might seem a stupid statement to say that wolves eat. The point is that although they are predators, they are also scavengers. Possession of food is nine-tenths of the law. When there is a shortage of food, possession is ten-tenths of the law and they will defend their prize in the most ferocious and convincing manner. Dead birds, mice, fish washed up, all become the property of the wolf that finds them.

We often pride ourselves on being able to take our dog's food away while he is eating, but that is because our domestic dog is well fed and kept satiated. Let him go hungry for a few days and then try to take the food away, and you will see just how quickly dormant instincts can come to the fore. Leave a piece of steak unattended and within reach of your dog, and finders keepers becomes the order of the day.

F.   Foul

With any animal, what goes in, must come out. The young wolf soon learns to leave the sleeping area to defecate. Mum keeps the den site clean by eating the cubs' droppings. This coprophagic behaviour is sometimes learnt by the youngster through a process of 'monkey see monkey do'. Dogs behave in exactly the same manner. Wolves have no problem with den-training; until they are old enough to wander away from the den, providing they do not soil where they sleep, anywhere else is OK. Our puppies learn the same thing, therefore going in the middle of your kitchen floor is the right thing to do from their point of view. Along comes the human, with a completely different set of values, and starts to confuse the whole issue. Instead of greeting the puppy and then cleaning the site — as would happen in a wolf den — he or she becomes angry and very often violent.

As the young wolf matures, leaving the den to defecate and urinate happens naturally. Given the opportunity, the same process happens with our young dogs. The cruel and barbaric 'old wives' tale' practice of rubbing their noses in the mess that they have made only teaches them to fear and mistrust us. The problem is that because our dogs eventually learn to go outside, people believe that this method works. The fact that they would have done this naturally does not cross their minds.

G. Growl

Like barking and biting, growling and snarling are natural expressive behaviour. Whereas barking is a call for back-up, growling is a clear-cut warning that an all-out attack is imminent if the intruder does not back down. The fact that a warning is issued in itself suggests that the wolf would rather not have to resort to a physical confrontation. A wolf pack is an extremely social group in which, contrary to popular opinion, actual violence between members happens quite rarely. Growling therefore is the audible warning, but what is more important is the facial expression that accompanies the growl. These expressions are varied and are intended to portray the emotional state of the growler.

Briefly, if the ears are flattened and the lips pulled back horizontally to form the submissive grin, the message is — I am frightened and will defend myself if I have to. If the ears are forward, hackles raised and the corners of the mouth pushed forward whilst the lips are retracted vertically, the message is — it is my intention to attack if you do not back down.

Wolf to wolf and dog to dog, this aggressive communication is understood. When our pet dog displays the same behaviour towards us, we take the view that 'no dog's gonna growl at me' and go forward to punish him. The result is invariably a bite and the dog is accused of being an aggressive animal — in fact it is we who are the aggressors.

H. Howl

I would imagine that of all the behaviour patterns exhibited by the wolf, its howl is the most well known. Most people are able to conjure up a picture of the lone wolf on a hilltop, apparently howling at the moon. Not so many people are aware of the group howl that precedes a hunting foray. In both cases it is a signal for others to gather round — a call for company.

Some dogs that have been isolated will howl. These dogs are usually over-attached to their human pack members and therefore cannot stand the desolation of being left alone whilst the rest of the pack go off hunting (as they see it). The howl of the wolf and the howl of the dog are both an eerie and heart-rending sound. It is probably the most expressive of the emotion-transmitting behaviours displayed by both species.

I.   Instinctive

To the wolf, survival is the name of the game. Other than their play-fighting, tug-of-war and the chase games that they engage upon with their litter brothers and sisters — all of which are designed to teach them hunting skills — they do not have any schooling. Their behaviour is inbred and totally instinctive. I recently saw film of a pack of fifteen wolves crossing a snow-covered terrain. Except for one or two slight pecking order battles taking place at the rear of the column, they were travelling in single file and in order of rank. As I watched, I recall thinking: that's the wolf equivalent of heelwork; not one of them had been to wolf club and none of them were wearing choke chains. If the instincts of the wolf lie dormant in our domestic dogs, why do we have so much trouble trying to stop them from pulling on the lead? Surely, if they regard us as being of higher rank, they should instinctively allow us to precede them. If they do not regard us as higher in rank, surely the instinct will be to lead. When viewed in this light, perhaps we are wasting our time with lessons designed to teach our dogs not to pull. Deep down, in the instincts inherited from their wolf forefathers, they should know where they should be walking.

J.   Jumping up

When the adult female wolf returns from a hunt, her cubs rush out to meet her, jumping up to lick at her lips. The sole purpose of this is to get her to regurgitate some of the partly digested food that she has eaten — a sort of baby food for wolves.

This is how wolves wean their cubs onto adult food. Lip-licking is also a gesture of submission and can be seen exhibited by the cubs shortly after they have been disciplined by mum. She will initially ignore their attempts by turning her head, but unless told to stop it, the cubs continue to jump up to reach her mouth. Our puppies exhibit exactly the same behaviour but, because we are upright creatures, they cannot reach our mouths unless we bend down and allow them to do so. The next time your puppy digs its needle-sharp teeth into your hand, try letting out a loud yelp of pain and then turn your head away — you will find that the puppy will try to lick your lips as a gesture of appeasement.

As the wolf matures, the games that it plays, as well as having a learning effect, are also designed to establish dominance/submissive levels between themselves and their counterparts.

Height reinforces rank, so the object is to place their paws on the shoulders or withers of their sparring partner. As you can see, what starts off as a food-soliciting/submissive behaviour, eventually progresses to being a dominant gesture. If the truth were known, we are flattered by our puppy's attempts to jump up at us, convinced that it is a display of affection. As our dog becomes more adult, we still believe that he is jumping up to greet us. If it starts to get out of hand, or the dog is muddy and we are dressed to go out, we often use aggressive methods to try and curb the behaviour. By this time, however, the transition from submissive to dominant gesture has taken place. If the dog is trying to dominate you and you become aggressive, you are accepting his challenge and sometimes the consequences are not very nice.

K. Kill

Wolves are killers! Very efficient, totally ruthless killing machines — they have to be to survive.

As a pack, they can travel at a steady gait for days on end, stopping only for the occasional rest. At the end of this tiring journey, they can hunt out and bring down a victim many times their own body weight. They need to hunt large game so that there is sufficient food for the whole pack, and when you consider that a hungry adult wolf can eat up to forty-four pounds of meat in a twenty-four hour period, you can see how efficient they have to be.

The dental arrangement of both wolves and dogs is the same. In other words, our cute, cuddly poodle that is fast asleep on our lap is a perfectly equipped killer. Obviously, by keeping the domestic dog in a relatively contained and comfortable environment, where it is well fed, and in a lot of cases overfed, these instincts are not aroused. However, if our dogs become cold and hungry and have the opportunity to form into a feral pack, they will kill to eat if they have to. The livestock losses that farmers suffer every year as a result of stray or uncontrolled dogs bears out their inherent instinct.

L. Lick

Licking is a behaviour that wolves practise for various reasons. The mother will lick her cubs to groom them and to stimulate urination and defecation, so that she can swallow the waste and maintain the cleanliness of the sleeping area before her cubs are strong enough to leave it.

Lip-licking remains a submissive gesture throughout the wolf's life, as does the licking of another wolf's genitals. However, licking as a mutual grooming session does occur but is usually initiated by the higher ranking and is therefore considered to be a dominant but highly social gesture. It is more often seen in the female of the species but it is not restricted to them — in the male, it is quite often the prelude to dominant mounting behaviour. The idea that dogs lick us because they are trying to get the salt off our skins is rarely the reason. More often than not, it is an attention-seeking behaviour — probably having its roots in the puppy's submissive licking gesture, to which we responded because we were flattered by its so-called affection.

The puppy is rewarded by the feed-back that it gets from us, and as it grows older the behaviour becomes dominant. Very few of us would scold a dog for what we saw as a display of affection. In other words, we respond to its grooming initiative on demand.

M. Mounting
Sexually orientated mounting behaviour must be the ultimate dominant position in any species. When it comes to wolves it is a clear-cut expression of rank. Mother nature dictates, depending upon the weather conditions and availability of food, just how many females will be capable of producing offspring. These females will be selected from the highest ranks, as will their male suitors. It follows, therefore, that having the right to mate is in itself a clear indication of rank.

Mounting is similar to jumping up, in that it involves the placing of paws on top of the other animal and therefore can be seen during play fights — whether these be male to male or female to female. It is exhibited for two reasons: firstly, to procreate, totally dependent on social status; secondly, to dominate, by achieving the top position but with no sexual intent.

It is not unusual for both male and female dogs to exhibit mounting behaviour during the onset of puberty. Not only is their system experiencing a tremendous hormone surge, but they are also psychologically going through a seniority classification period — trying to establish some sort of position within the mixed canine/human pack. Invariably, they will grow out of it as the hormones settle, but only if you have established your position as the Alpha figure. If this has been achieved and the behaviour continues, usually having the dog or bitch neutered cures the problem.

When you consider that, in a wolf pack, only the highest-ranking females come into season and then only once a year, whereas the majority of domestic female dogs come into season twice a year and, increasingly, three times a year, it goes to show that our advanced knowledge of canine nutrition is probably creating a need for a spaying and neutering programme. What mother nature does naturally and is policed instinctively, we have to do surgically.

N.   Natural behaviour

A dog might show many of the behaviour patterns of a wolf, but these behaviours have been tempered through selective breeding and generations of domestication. Therefore, although a dog might often act like a tame wolf, a wolf will rarely act like a tame dog.

There is an increasing trend amongst some dog people to want to own a wolf or a wolf hybrid, a practice which I feel is totally irresponsible considering the growing anti-dog lobby at large in this country today. There are wolf societies already in existence and I am sure that their members are responsible people who know about the nature of the wolf and keep their charges under the proper conditions. My fear, though, is that wolf ownership will get out of hand in this country as it has done in America. Even one that has been hand reared will still have the wild temperament of wolves. They have a tendency to be overfearful when faced with unfamiliar objects or people, and their fight-or-flight instincts are often over-reactive. If you inadvertently block the flight path of an animal of such size and speed, then a fear bite might result. Make no mistake, although the dental characteristics of both dogs and wolves are similar, the wolf is by far the more powerful animal and his teeth are much bigger. The simple act of placing a suitcase on the kitchen floor will solicit investigation from the domestic dog; it could well send a wolf into a blind panic.

It is likely that in a litter of wolf hybrids, some will inherit the calmer and less reactive temperament of the dog, whilst the rest will inherit the wild and unpredictable temperament of the wolf. The owner who gets the latter will begin to see behaviour changes in the form of distinct wild traits at around four-and-a-half to five months of age, and he or she might become dangerous during the breeding season. Even a hybrid with a fairly stable temperament will have the activity level, exploratory nature and natural clumsiness of the wolf — having him in the house for a day will be like having ten (three-year-old) children for a week. Kept outside in a large enclosure with other wolves, or with dogs that he has been raised with, then a good relationship with mutual affection can be achieved — providing he is always treated with respect for what he is.

A dog is a pet that is related to, and exhibits similar behaviour to, the wolf. A wolf will always be a wolf.

O.   Omnivorous

Although the staple diet of a wolf is meat, it is not a strict carnivore and is capable of digesting a certain amount of vegetable protein. The majority of wolf kills are made on herbivorous animals and the whole animal is eaten, including the stomach contents both digested and undigested.

The diet of wolves is obviously dependent on food availability, and at times they have to eke out a scavenging existence. During these periods they will eat fruit, vegetables, rotten meat — in fact, anything that they can get hold of. But this is not of their choosing, it is simply a question of survival, and their digestive system has developed to enable them to extract whatever nutrients they can from a variety of different food sources. When food is abundant, they are primarily meat eaters and it is on this diet that they fare the best. Our dogs have the same digestive system, and although it is probably very 'green' to be a vegetarian, I think that it is unfair to inflict our standards and social conscience on our dogs. Vegetarian diets can be given to dogs and, no doubt, dogs will survive on them. But mother nature designed their system for just that — to survive when the going gets tough. To thrive, in my view, they need a correctly balanced diet that contains a good quality meat protein. Whether we eat meat or not is our choice. Given the same choice, wolves eat meat.

P.   Pack animals

Over the centuries, wolves have been persecuted, hunted and killed almost to the point of extinction — this on the basis that they were evil killers of humans. In reality, the wolf is rarely aggressive to people — curiosity and fear would best describe its behaviour towards us.

At one time the wolf was the most widely distributed land mammal in the world. But through the myths and legends that have surrounded it, in the minds of people it became an animal to be feared. The popular medieval view linked it with the devil — there has always been talk of werewolves, half-man, half-wolf, but I have never heard a story about a good one. Children have been brought up to fear the wolf, with stories of Little Red Riding Hood who was waylaid by an extremely intelligent, extremely cruel creature.

Perhaps man does have good reason to fear the wolf — not because it is evil, but because as a group its social structure is similar to ours but works better because it lacks the human destructive emotions of greed, envy and revenge. As humans, we seem to have to be the ultimate animal — rather than learn, we destroy. Over the last few decades, attitudes have thankfully been changing and the wolf is now being studied more than hunted; as a result, it is once again on the increase.

These studies are showing just how social wolves are as a group. One photographer, who spent a summer watching wolves in the high Arctic, was led to comment, 'I've never seen animals that have so many characteristics that can be felt — no wonder early people chose wolves as companions.' They generally live in manageable groups of under ten (although a pack of thirty-six was once recorded in Alaska). They have a hierarchical structure which, in a large, well-established pack, will include an upper, middle and lower class. The upper classes would include the Alpha male and female, the middle classes generally consist of non-breeding adults and the lower classes would include any outcasts and youngsters under two years of age.

This rank structure is maintained not through displays of aggression, but through displays of deference towards their peers. Quite often there will be a group display of active submission towards the Alpha male, designed to confirm his status and the group's solidarity as a unit. The overriding atmosphere is one of friendliness and mutual loyalty.

When you consider that if a female has cubs, other females will produce milk in case anything happens to the natural mother, we can begin to see that a wolf pack is a self-help, co-operative, consistently stable, social society. Wouldn't it be nice if our human society could follow suit and live year in, year out with one common aim — the greater good of the group. This is what probably attracted us to wolves in the first place. This is probably why we resented and feared them for centuries, because they had achieved what we would like to achieve. This is the instinctive commitment that their cousins, our dogs, have towards the pack in which they live today.

Q.   Quarrel

Having painted a picture of domestic bliss within a wolf pack, it would be ridiculous to pretend that there are not occasional disputes between them. However, because their social structure is so clearly defined, these quarrels happen rarely and once they have sorted them out, life continues with no grudges being borne.

It might surprise you to learn that the dominant male rarely shows any aggression towards the members of his pack, in fact the opposite is true. In general, the Alpha male is surprisingly tolerant and friendly towards his subordinates and this is because his position is well established. He walks tall and looks all others directly in the eye, with the attitude of 'I make the decisions and they are not open to discussion'. Any disputes happen lower down the pecking order, with the biggest culprits being numbers two and three in a dominance battle for the position of pack leader elect. These quarrels are usually over very quickly and, although frightening to watch because of the ferocity involved, very rarely result in much damage being done to either party.

As predators and part of a hunting unit, they instinctively know that if they get injured themselves they will be unable to join the hunt. If they injure the other party, the effectiveness of the pack as a hunting unit will be reduced. As a result, these disputes are resolved through displays of aggression rather than out-and-out aggression with the intention of maiming and disabling the opponent. Our dogs behave in much the same way if we allow them to do so. Unfortunately we seldom do; we interfere, and it is through this that injuries occur — invariably to us.

R.   Regurgitate

Wolves are vomiting animals. We have already discussed the fact that the cubs will lick the lips of the returning female in order to get her to regurgitate food. We have also discussed the fact that they are capable of existing on a varied diet which sometimes includes rotting flesh. Anything that starts to upset the wolf's digestive system, including parasites, can be expelled through the eating of certain grasses — as opposed to animals that are incapable of regurgitating and who therefore have to suffer the consequences of selecting the wrong food.

Basically, the ability to dispel food at will is a survival mechanism cleverly designed by mother nature. As with all other behaviours, our dogs have the same ability which they exercise on a regular basis. Providing it is not a daily occurrence, or starts to happen on a multiple basis that does not appear to be self-induced, then it is perfectly normal behaviour.

S. Scent mark

The olfactory system (sense of smell) of the wolf is a truly amazing piece of machinery. It lives in a world which is full of airborne information, many times more sophisticated than the information that we transmit verbally over the airways. A brief sniff at a ground scent left by an animal will tell the wolf what species it is, its state of health, and in which direction it was heading. This ability allows wolves to use scent to transmit information between themselves and to neighbouring wolf packs.

These messages are passed on in a chemical form called pheromones which — unlike hormones which are secreted internally — are secreted externally. A female in season will secrete pheromones in her urine which will sexually arouse males. Both males and females (but mainly males) will deposit pheromone signals, mainly through the urine and faeces but it is thought also through the foot pads, as a way of marking out territory, hence the ground scratching after urination — a sort of invisible post-coding of property as practised by human neighbourhood watch groups. The 'pheromone effect' is designed to influence the behaviour of other animals of the same species, either as a warning to stay away, or as an invitation to stick around. The scent-marking behaviour of the wolf is a very complex and inter-species-recognised form of communication. Pheromones are used by many different life forms, from insects upwards; but none of them uses this chemical language as effectively and to portray such a wide variety of different meanings as does the wolf. The chemical signals that are

I smell pheromones!

transmitted are generally well advertised, which is one of the reasons why dogs cock their legs — the object being to deposit their scent as high as possible so that the air currents can transmit it in all directions. Some very male-orientated bitches will also use this leg-cocking technique, even though it is more usual for them to squat to urinate. Bitches that exhibit this behaviour are generally very high ranking within the group, as are the prolific leg-cocking males. It would seem, therefore, that the right to post a notice of intent is largely dependent upon rank.

The modern dog is no different. Because of selective breeding, we now have some dogs that are a fraction of the size of the original blue-print. It is not unusual to see a female member of one of the smaller breeds, in particular the dominant terrier variety, standing on her forelegs and depositing urine in short sharp squirts onto a vertical object. This is not a need to urinate, it is a need to communicate: the human equivalent of a verbal warning, a written warning, a telephone warning or, more recently, a faxed warning. It might also be some sort of invitation, but in the absence of their incredible olfactory abilities, we can only guess.

T.   Territorial

Wolves are fiercely territorial creatures and each pack will mark out its hunting territory by urinating and defecating on prominent landmarks around the boundaries. As we have just discussed, the message in these territory marks is transmitted through the pheromones. They are also great respecters of territory, and when travelling from one hunting ground to another will detour many miles rather than encroach upon the hunting territory of another pack. Scientists who have studied wolf behaviour have observed from spotter planes that if a pack of wolves chases an intended victim across the boundary of another pack, they will give up the chase and leave the spoils of their hard work to the resident group. It would have to be an extremely hungry pack to break these lupine laws.

Our dogs are also territorial creatures, but because society demands that they should also be sociable, the canine laws have evolved in a slightly different way. The 'no go' areas are generally our houses and gardens, and woe betide any canine intruder who trespasses. The smallest resident will successfully chase off the largest intruder, basically because the intruder knows that he should not be there. Even introducing a human-accompanied dog onto the territory of another can be a tricky business. Not always will a fight occur, but there will certainly be a great deal of meaningful body language between them.

The main difference is that there are also communal territories — the parks and fields where different dogs are exercised on a daily basis. One of the reasons why this can happen is that each dog thinks that it is trespassing on the territory of another, and because none of them considers that it has any right to defend, they all generally act in a more submissive way. The body postures would portray the message, 'I am not here of my own free will and I do not intend to challenge your right to be here'; with all the dogs transmitting the same message, there will generally be no trouble.

Problems can arise, though, where a dog is not allowed to interact regularly with others, especially when it is young. Lack of early socialisation on communal territory will mean that the dog never learns that there are such areas. His wolf instinct will take over and, if he is allowed to stake out boundaries, he will defend them. Two dogs from different houses, which are exercised regularly on the same territory and allowed to mark the same boundaries each time, will fight for the right to be there if they ever meet.

Dogs whose owners have large gardens and think that the dog will get enough exercise without going off territory, will become very aggressive towards other dogs who come anywhere near their boundaries — sometimes even towards humans. Fence-running and constant barking are common problems with these dogs, to say nothing of the aggression.

U.   Urinate

Of course wolves urinate, as do all animals that need to get rid of excess fluid, but here is where the similarity ends. Wolves also urinate to mark territory, as we have already established, and they urinate as a sign of submission. It is this last behaviour that we are going to look at here.

Submissive urination is a reflex action learnt at an early stage when the adult female would gently turn her cubs over and lick them to stimulate urination and defecation. The cub learns that being turned over is a dominant behaviour on the part of its mother, whilst lying on its back and urinating is a submissive behaviour. As it gets older, this behaviour is used to signify submission and acceptance of another's higher rank. It does not necessarily roll right over, but adopts a very low, crouching approach, as if it were about to roll over and deposit little squirts of urine. In the older wolf, lying on the back and urinating would signify total submission. The more confident the wolf becomes, the less likely it is to exhibit this behaviour, which would therefore suggest that the behaviour is not a deliberate signal but a conditioned reflex reaction triggered off by the animal's personal awareness of its own status. (In other words, it can't help it and is probably not even conscious that it is doing it.)

None of us is surprised when we see our puppies exhibit similar behaviour, but we get quite upset if our older dogs do the same thing. The problem here is that because the behaviour is an unconscious acceptance of the approach of a more dominant animal, the more upset we become, the more dominant we appear. Scolding the dog for piddling as it approaches is going to make it piddle even more.

In almost every case where this is the reported problem, there is a history of overly dominant early training programmes having been practised by the owner. Attempts to dominate the puppy as early as possible, and at a time when it automatically viewed the owner as the dominant animal, leads to an over-stimulation of this submissive expression of emotion. Confidence-building programmes and a reduction of dominant body postures on the part of the owner at the times when the dog is most likely to behave in this way are the only means to improve the problem.

V. Valueless

Wolves, or any other wild animal for that matter, do not view things in terms of monetary, social or aesthetic values. They rely totally on instincts and are not bogged down by right and wrong values. They do not preserve young trees for posterity as we might: if they need more fibre, up come the roots. If they are hungry, they kill whatever they can, regardless of how pretty it might look. We might swat a moth but rarely a butterfly.

We expect our dogs to understand our values and these are based mainly on monetary issues. We might not mind if we found that our dog had chewed up last week's newspaper, but we would hit the roof if we found that he had chewed up a £20 note. Chewing the leg of an old kitchen stool does not warrant as much punishment as chewing the leg of the Parker Knoll chair. These values are totally confusing to a dog because, like the wolf, if there is a need for something and it is there — take it. If there is a need for fibre and there is some already pulped and made into paper, then that'll do nicely. If the puppy is teething and there's something to chew on — chew it.

W. Whine

Whining is basically a distress call. A cub will whine if it is cold, hungry, away from its brothers and sisters, or because it can't find mum. It is one of the earliest vocalisations to develop and, just like human parents, the female wolf is totally tuned in to the distress calls of her cubs and will respond immediately. As they grow older, they become far more independent and, although whining remains a signal of distress, they do not expect the attention that they rapidly received when they were cubs.

Our dogs are rarely allowed to develop the same independence; to a certain extent they remain dependent upon us throughout their lives. For this reason, whining can become an attention-seeking problem behaviour because we continue to respond.

X.

This could refer to x-breeds but is more relevant to the dog than to the wolf. Wolves, on the whole, are pure-bred. Except where wolves have been raised and socialised with dogs from an early age, the chances of them mating are pretty remote — the wolf being more inclined to kill the dog than to make love to it. The relevance of this section is that because each breed of dog has been selectively bred for some inherited breed-specific behaviour — for example, herding, guarding, hunting — it is important that, wherever possible, the owner identifies the dog's genetic inheritance in terms of its likely behaviour so that he knows what to expect. Where this has not been possible, just by looking at the dog, especially of the Heinz 57 variety, by studying its behaviour a fairly accurate guess can be made about which group to place it in.

Interestingly, if you took the offspring of two different breeds and mated them with the offspring of two more different breeds, then repeated this procedure again and again, before long — except for its size — the dog would start to revert to type. The ears would be erect, the tail carried low, and the animal would become far more independent and not as easily trained. The type to which it is reverting is the wolf, and this is probably why most sightings of cross-bred strays report: breed unknown but definitely had some German Shepherd origins.

Y. Yelping
Another cry of distress, but limited to painful experiences or sudden surprise. Exhibited by both wolf and dog and totally self-explanatory.

Z. Zoonoses
These are diseases that can be passed from one species to another — wolf to dog, dog to man, wolf to man — the most dangerous being rabies. Listing these diseases would not be within the brief of this book. I have included this category for one reason only: if the wolf, the dog and the human have come so far as even to share diseases, then it must be the final seal on the bond between us.

Having read through this A to Z, you will realise that, in many of the questions raised in Part Three, the owner is actually complaining about behaviour which does not suit his life-style or personal values, although in almost all cases the problem is attributed to the dog. For sure, there are problem dogs, dogs that exhibit phobic and maladjusted behaviour; but in general their behaviour is entirely normal and inherited from their forefather, the wolf.

My task, therefore, is firstly to sort out the normal from the abnormal — where it is abnormal, to suggest a cure; where it is normal but unacceptable, to advise on how to channel it to suit the owner's individual needs. From this last statement it can be seen that problem behaviour is relevant to the owner. I quite often get calls from people who complain that their dog does . . . Now and again it goes through my mind, 'Well, so does mine, where's the problem?' But what one person can tolerate, another cannot, and finding out that the so-called 'expert' has a similar problem with one of his dogs does not instil a lot of confidence. The behaviour that the dog is exhibiting has reached a problematical level, as far as the owner is concerned, and he has called or written for advice. Telling him that he should tolerate it because I do is of no use to him. What follows is what I say instead.

Part Three

WHY DOES MY DOG . . . ?

In the following pages, we shall be looking at the various problems encountered by pet owners. These are all genuine questions which I have collected from a variety of sources and, occasionally, the advice will be repetitive because the root cause is the same. I feel sure that as you progress through them, before you read the answer you will begin to formulate your own ideas about how you would cure the problem. If what I advise is different from how you would tackle it, it does not necessarily mean that one of us is wrong. Providing the results are successful, then the method must have been correct.

WHY DOES MY DOG . . .

A

Abnormal

So far, what we have discussed shows that the majority of problems exhibited by dogs are usually perfectly normal behaviour, albeit totally unacceptable. Some dogs do, however, display abnormal behaviour, and when this occurs the prognosis for a cure is not good.

A recent example involved a three-year-old Dobermann bitch owned by a family which included two small children (three years and one year old). The dog had been obtained two months previously from a rescue society, because her original owners had divorced and neither of them was in a position to keep her. The problem was that the new mum was finding that she could not cope with the dog's activity level on top of her two small children.

Before meeting the dog, I had assumed that the problem was either lack of effective control or perhaps a diet-related hyperactivity. This preconceived idea proved to be totally wrong; the reason why she behaved in this way was a direct result of her early experiences with people. I knew this because fortunately the rescue kennels had given the new owners a full history of the dog, something that very rarely happens since the kennels are not always told the truth in the first place.

She was an only pup whose mother had died shortly after giving birth. She was therefore raised by humans and had no early contact with other dogs until she was able to go out into the big wide world. Knowing this, I correctly predicted that her behaviour towards other dogs would be one of avoidance, but where this was not possible she exhibited a freeze reflex (discussed on p. 69).

As a puppy she had learnt to identify with people, because they were her only contact through the critical periods of development known as the socialisation periods; in short, she had never learnt to be a dog.

Through a process known as imprinting, she had not only become overattached but, where physically possible, had adopted the behaviour patterns of people, particularly their activity level. Humans should be active by day, cats by night, whereas the dog's sleep patterns can vary throughout a twenty-four hour period. When there is nothing going on they sleep, but are immediately ready and active as soon as something interests them. With this particular dog, she was interested in everything the humans were doing and only rested when everyone else did. This meant that she was constantly under mum's feet, trying to involve herself with what she was doing. Understandably, with two small children behaving in pretty much the same way, mum frequently got quite tetchy with the dog, the kids and with dad when he got home.

The caring people who had gently hand-reared this Dobe bitch could not have foreseen that they would eventually affect the quality of life for another family. Had they known, they could have taught the puppy how to be a dog by letting it interact with other puppies and allowing an adult dog access to it at an early age. Dogs teach puppies how to behave and they need not be related to accept the responsibility; provided there is also human contact, they quickly learn how to be dogs in a domestic environment. The importance of proper early experience cannot be stressed enough if the puppy is to behave in a normal manner when it matures. Lack of early experience is ONE of the causes of abnormal behaviour, and how problematical this becomes depends entirely upon the circumstances of the environment that inherits the dog. In this case, the situation was intolerable – mum was on her way to a nervous breakdown and the dog, the kids and dad were suffering as a result.

This particular case had a happy ending. We were able to re-home the dog with an active retired couple who appreciated the problem but felt that they could easily cope with and enjoy the company of a people-orientated dog. The problem dealt with below, however, does not have such a happy ending.

Question
We have a six-year-old male Bulldog which has recently become very aggressive towards other dogs or bitches and puppies. This started about six weeks ago but appears to be get-

ting worse to the point that he recently attacked a German Shepherd bitch who managed to escape and run away. This did not stop our dog's aggression, however; he continued to fight with himself, seemingly oblivious to the fact that the other dog had gone. Neither myself nor the owner of the German Shepherd dog could believe what we were seeing. He had his back leg in his mouth, his eyes were glazed and he refused to let go. When he did eventually calm down, he had injured himself quite badly. On three or four occasions over the last two weeks he has growled at our ten-year-old son for no apparent reason. This is such a change in his behaviour from how he has been since he was a puppy. He loved to play with other dogs and I would have trusted him completely with children.

Answer
It is usually encouraging when the changes in behaviour happen well into adulthood, because it signifies that there is a cause rather than a temperament fault, and if this cause can be established a cure can usually be found. In this case, I fear the worst. Fighting in the absence of an opponent is definitely abnormal behaviour, which suggests that the aggression has gone out of control. What worries me is the onset of aggressive behaviour towards your son who might not be as nimble on his feet as the German Shepherd was. Whenever there is a report of aggression towards children, I always err on the side of caution. All the time that we spend in trying to modify the behaviour of the dog, the children are at risk and neither you nor I could forgive ourselves if your child was attacked at a later date because we failed to heed the warnings. Considering the age of the dog at the time of the change in behaviour, the dramatic turn-about in his temperament, the ferocity of his aggression with a noticeable change in his pupil dilatory level and the fact that the behaviour has become abnormal would all suggest that the problem is neurological. I strongly advise you to seek veterinary advice before you take any other course of action. (Post script. The owners did seek veterinary advice and euthanasia was advised. A post mortem revealed a brain tumour.)

This second example shows that another major cause of abnormal behaviour is illness, which is one of the reasons why I, and my colleagues in the APBC, work strictly on veterinary referral. By doing so, we can assume that the dog has had a medical work-up before being referred. In this case, the owners had been advised to contact me before the aggressive confrontation with the German Shepherd. There were no physical clues to the condition that the dog was suffering from because brain tumours obviously cannot be seen with the naked eye. Although the outcome was sad, the owners were lucky that the problem manifested itself in such a bizarre way, prompting urgent medical attention. Had it been a more subtle change which remained within the bounds of normal but unacceptable behaviour, we might have been tempted to try a programme of rehabilitation which would certainly have resulted in disaster.

Aggression

This is a major subject which would warrant a book on its own. There are many causes of aggression and more and more labels are being concocted to explain the different types. Nervous aggression, pain-associated aggression, rage syndrome, territorial aggression — I have even heard of one called strobo-scopic aggression, being attributed to breeds like the Old English or Bearded Collie which have hair covering their eyes. I suspect that we could work through the alphabet and find a type of aggression to cover each letter, but at the end of the day, what does aggression mean? It means that the dog either barks at, growls at, or bites people or other animals. As I explained in Part Two, this is normal.

I intend, therefore, to include the more relevant 'types' of aggression within the alphabetical list — for example, if you consider your dog to be a nervous aggressive type, turn to the 'N' chapter for a comparative question and answer. But before you go winging your way towards your categorised aggression problem, it will help if you understand the problem as a whole.

Aggression is usually a defence reflex, initially exhibited as a threat or warning, ultimately exhibited in a real form when there is no other option left. In other words, it can usually be avoided if you understand the cause, can read the signs and know how to desensitise the dog's lack of trust towards the situation that resulted in the aggressive confrontation — nearly all aggression results from a lack of trust on the part of the dog.

In general terms, dogs exhibit three defence reflexes: active defence reflexes (ADR), passive defence reflexes (PDR) and freeze reflex (FR). What this really means is that if they feel threatened they will either bite you, run away, or enter an almost catatonic state of immobility. If you think about it, humans exhibit the same behaviour patterns when they feel threatened, as do most animals.

The freeze reflex is probably the least common in dogs. Having said that, I recall a story told me by someone who had undergone a Home Office Course to qualify as a professional dog handler. Armed with this certificate, he offered his services as a private dog trainer on a part-time basis. His first client was a woman with a Pyrenean Mountain Dog that pulled her on the lead. Based upon the training he had received, he put a choke chain around the dog's neck and started to walk. The dog immediately started to forge forward and this 'trainer' shouted HEEL and yanked the chain. The dog froze and no amount of coaxing or forcing would make it move: they were in the middle of a busy public park with a ten-stone breathing statue. To cut a long story short, they had to fetch a car to the dog and, between them, lift the dog into it. The dog remained in this state until the trainer was out of sight; the moment he reappeared, the dog resumed his catatonic state. The only heart-warming part of this story was the trainer's final comments: 'I was so embarrassed that I shall never offer private lessons again.'

Active defence reflexes are probably the most common reason for the popular diagnosis 'aggressive dog'. Unlike the last example, when ADR dogs feel threatened, they defend themselves in the only way they know how to — they growl, snarl and eventually will bite. Dogs with passive defence reflexes will prefer to run away and hide.

Although there are variations within each breed, some breeds like the Rottweiler, Jack Russell, Japanese Akita, and others, would generally display active defence reflexes. Golden Retrievers, Shelties and dogs of that ilk would basically have passive defence reflexes. These are traits which have been encouraged through selective breeding depending upon the job the dog was originally intended to perform — it would be no good breeding for guarding purposes a dog that exhibited PDR.

So it can be seen that, providing there is no other factor which is causing the aggression, dogs will not initiate aggression unless provoked. Our journey into their wolf ancestry has shown that they are basically very social creatures which will resort to an aggressive confrontation only as a last resort, but some breeds are more likely to react aggressively

than others. These could be classified as 'low threshold aggressive breeds', whereas 'high threshold aggressive breeds' will
only react when escape is not possible — assuming they don't
freeze instead. The best way of describing the dog's defence
mechanism is to remember the three 'F's — Fight, Flight or
Freeze.

Hereditary temperament problems, aggressive training
techniques, lack of early socialisation, diet, illness and pain are
just some of the factors that can be involved in altering the level
of threshold at which a dog will react. When considering the
aggressive behaviour of a dog, therefore, we should bear in
mind three things:

1   The particular breed's normal defence reflex.
2   The factors that provoke this reflex.
3   The factors that might be lowering the threshold.

Agoraphobia

Just as some people have a genuine fear of open spaces, some
dogs can suffer from the same complaint. The root cause can
often be traced back to a traumatic experience that happened
outside the safety of its familiar environment when the pup was
between eight and twelve weeks old. During this period, sometimes called the fear imprint period, anything that frightens the
pup can have a lasting, often phobic effect for the rest of its life.
It may have experienced pain at the vet's, or it may have been
frightened by the loud hiss of air brakes on a large lorry, or even
had its foot trodden on by a big fat man wearing a black coat
and sunglasses. At best, the puppy will develop a long-lasting
fear of vets, lorries, or big fat men in black coats who wear sunglasses. At worst, it might generalise these experiences to being
outside the house, and so the problem arises. Although it is
important to socialise puppies as early as possible, the owner
should take great pains to ensure that nothing traumatic happens during this time. If this is the cause of agoraphobic
behaviour in your dog, then a careful programme of
desensitisation needs to be worked out, and to do this properly
you will need to ask your vet to refer you to a behaviourist. It
might also pay dividends to get referred to a homoeopathic vet
who will be able to treat your dog for specific fears without
resorting to drugs.

Question

I have a two-year-old Retriever bitch who until recently loved to play in the garden. A few weeks ago, a large airship passed over the house and obviously frightened her. Since then, all she does when we open the door for her is stand in the open doorway and look upwards. No amount of coaxing will get her to go out, and the only way we can get her to relieve herself is to put her lead on in the house, put her straight into the car and take her to the park. In the park she appears to be fine, but as soon as we get home she bolts out of the car and can't wait to get back into the house. Is she suffering from agoraphobia?

Answer

Not in the true sense. Her fear is environmental rather than in general. I suspect that her behaviour has also been inadvertently encouraged: first, through your attempts to coax her outside, which could be construed by her as praise (come on, there's a good girl, it's OK); next, by your increased off-territory exercise routine because you fear that she must be bursting to go to the loo, and the park is more exciting than the garden as far as she is concerned. Therefore, what started off as a very real fear quickly became a learned behaviour because it started to bring her reward.

You need to ignore her completely when she goes through her 'I couldn't possibly go out there' routine — don't look at her, don't speak to her. Leave the door open for her as much as possible and let her make the decisions. If she has been properly house-trained, she will nip outside if she needs to rather than soil the house, and this can be rewarded with a tit-bit (outside, not when she comes back in). If she is fed once a day, increase her mealtimes to twice a day — the same daily amount, split into two portions. Mix it in her presence and, without saying anything, put it outside the door. Let her think about it for fifteen minutes and if she hasn't gone out to eat it, throw it away. Repeat the procedure at each meal and don't worry, a fit, healthy dog will not starve to death.

If she likes her visit to the park, pick up her lead but don't put her on it, and walk to the car. If she doesn't follow you, go back and shut her in the house. Drive round the block and return — she will only get her park exercise when she follows you out of the house of her own free will. All daily tit-bit routines should be given outside the house, and if she refuses to come out for them she doesn't get them. Basically what you should be doing is stopping all rewards inside the house, including your gentle coaxing, and adopting an off-hand attitude towards her behaviour. All rewards will be transferred to outside the house, but only when she leaves of her own free will — taking her out on a lead does not allow her the choice. Lastly, keep your eyes peeled for airships; if you see one in the distance, get her inside quick, before she sees it.

Anorexia nervosa

If a dog that usually has a healthy appetite starts refusing to eat, get it to your vet. Until your vet proves otherwise, this should always be treated as a medical problem first. If, however, there proves to be nothing wrong with the dog, then we can assume that it is canine anorexia nervosa — a psychological problem.

Dogs that suffer from this are not like people — if dogs get fat they don't care. They don't pretend to eat food and then secretly regurgitate it. They don't eat to be polite and then scourge their systems with laxatives — they just don't eat. In almost every case, this is a result of some trauma and is completely different from the finicky eating patterns of some dogs, especially the more pampered toy breeds. The finicky eaters usually worry their owners by hardly eating enough to keep a fly alive, when in fact they probably have a very low metabolic rate and don't need as much food as the owners think they do. Often they have learnt to play the game 'I can't eat that, it's dog food — give me a steak'; their reward is that the owner usually does. Another good ruse is 'how to get attention' and lots of picky eaters end up being hand fed. These dogs are not anorexic, they are usually just brats.

Complete refusal to eat is fairly rare and usually environmental. For example, I recently dealt with a case where the dog had not eaten for five days. Veterinary examination showed that there was nothing physically wrong with him. A step-by-step account of the incidents that occurred on the day that he stopped eating eventually produced the answer. He was always fed in the same place in the kitchen. To the right of where he ate was a loose baby gate which was used to prop against the open door leading into the lounge to stop the dog pestering the family when they ate in there. On this particular day the gate had been knocked over and had fallen on the dog. No one had given this incident a second thought, but obviously the effect was pretty traumatic to the dog. We moved his food bowl outside and he started to eat greedily. Before he finished it all, we brought the bowl back into the kitchen and he refused to eat. We left the bowl where it was and moved the baby gate outside: the dog finished his meal.

Question
I have a two-year-old Yorkshire Terrier which has always been a fussy eater. Recently we put him into kennels for the first time and in the two weeks that he was there he didn't eat a thing. He came out looking like skin and bones and the kennel owner has said that he is anorexic (the dog, not the kennel owner). My vet does not agree because when we got him home he started to eat again. My question is, what should we do if we want to go away again?

Answer
First of all I would find a different kennels. Any kennel owner who allows a dog to go for two weeks without eating and does not call a vet should not be running kennels. What you describe is indeed anorexia nervosa, caused through kennel stress. The fact that your dog is not a good eater in general suggests that he is a pretty much loved and, if you were to be honest, a slightly spoiled dog. The trauma that he experienced by being isolated in a noisy kennel environment for the first time was almost the same as some of the experimentally induced behavioural problems experienced by scientists engaged upon studies into conditioned reflexes. With *some* dogs, even the mildest electric shock created psychological trauma, with fits, aggression, hyperactive behaviour and refusal to eat being some of the symptoms.

My advice would be to try and create a less attached relationship with your dog. I don't mean that you should love him any the less, just that he should not be so dependent upon you all the time. If you have to use kennels when you go away, I should consult your vet first. He *may* be able to recommend a kennel (*see* Boarding, p. 86) that can deal with this sort of problem and he may even prescribe a mild sedative to help the dog settle in. But why put your dog through the trauma in the first place? He has shown everyone that he cannot psychologically handle this sort of environment, and there are some animals that truly can't. Why don't you suggest to one of your dog's friends' owners that you will look after their dog when they go away, if they will look after yours when you go away? Alternatively, there are people who will look after your house and pets when you go away, but make sure you get a first-hand recommendation first.

Anthropomorphism

This means attributing human form or personality to animals, and no book about dogs would be complete without using this word at least once. Of all the domestic pets, the dog is the one that is granted human status and human powers of reasoning. I know that many cat owners treat their cats like child substitutes, but the cat has an aloofness that allows it to rise above all of this and so, deep down, we still respect it as a cat. Not so the dog: the humans around it become mummies and daddies, brothers and sisters, uncles and aunties, and we take great pains not to hurt the dog's feelings. Dogs are extremely clever at exploiting this relationship, by exhibiting body postures and facial expressions that convince us that they are sulking and upset about what we have said or done. This further adds to our beliefs that they have the same reasoning powers as ourselves.

They don't of course, they are dogs — just as cats are cats. Dogs don't sulk, they show respect by not getting in your way. They don't get excited because it's Christmas morning and there are lots of presents under the tree for them, they just react to the general air of goodwill, the fun and the change in the normal routine. But the thing that upsets many of my clients is to be told that their dog does not come to them for a cuddle

And if you are very good while I'm out I'll let you watch TV when I get back.

when they are watching television because it loves them so much, it does it to demand attention.

A classic example of this anthropomorphic attitude was portrayed recently on television in a comedy vet series. The client brought her two toy dogs to the vet in a pram, complaining that the female was getting fat and acting rather strangely. The vet examined her and said she was pregnant.

'That cannot be,' said the client, 'she hasn't been near another dog.'

'What about this one?' asked the vet, pointing to the other dog in the pram, a male.

'Don't be disgusting, young man,' said the client, 'that's her brother.'

Question

Why does my dog always punish me when I pick her up from the kennels after I have been on holiday? It is a lovely kennel and they are very good to her, but when we bring her back home she ignores us as if she is angry with us. What can I do to bring her round?

Answer

Absolutely nothing! I think you are making the mistake of assuming that dogs have similar emotions to humans — in this case anger and a desire to punish. They don't. What you are seeing is the effect upon a dog that is generally placed upon a pedestal and granted privileges which, if it were a feral dog (wild dog), would be granted only to the highest ranking. Kennelling such dogs is a form of isolation and effectively reduces their status. When they return home, and until they manage to climb back up the pecking order ladder, they will display all the canine body postures of the under-dog within your canine/human pack. They are unobtrusive. If called, they will approach with a low head carriage and will avert eye contact. They will not initiate any play activity and they will hang back slightly when you go through doorways and narrow passageways.

My advice would be to take a long, hard look at your dog's behaviour prior to going into kennels. If I have described correctly what you call punishment and anger, then for 50 weeks of the year she has got the wrong impression of her role within your environment.

Anxiety

Having said that dogs do not have the same reasoning powers as humans, they do indeed have the ability to develop strong emotional attachments and can suffer from psychosomatic disorders similar to those suffered by people. As we have seen, anorexia nervosa is one such example and is in fact anxiety-related. The emotional and autonomic nervous system is very similar in organisation to that which is found in the human brain; the difference lies in some of the ways in which dogs express their anxiety.

Most commonly seen anxiety-related problems are: house-soiling; destructiveness; escape behaviour (digging near doors and windows); howling and barking and, in severe cases, self-mutilation.

In almost every case, the problem manifests itself when the owners leave the dog in the house on its own. The dog becomes anxious and the manifested problems are ways of relieving the tension that this anxiety creates. The exact form of the tension-relieving behaviour will depend upon the individual dog: an introvert will be more likely to self-mutilate (direct its tension inwards), whereas an extrovert will be more inclined to destroy things (direct its tension on to something else).

Whenever I am told that the owner's dog exhibits one of these problems, I always ask the same questions.

Does the dog follow you from room to room?
Does it sleep in the bedroom?
Does it try and get into the lavatory with you?
Does it scratch or cry and howl when doors are accidentally shut on it?
Is it always flopped down at your feet whenever you sit down, usually with one paw over your feet, or does it insist on sitting on your lap?

If the answer to these questions is yes, I know that we are talking about an over-attached relationship and the problems have arisen because the dog cannot stand the desolation of being left alone. Obtaining another dog is not the answer to this problem because it is not loneliness that causes it — it is people that the dog craves for and usually one particular person in the house.

The prognosis for curing an anxiety-related problem is very good. Because we know what the root cause is, we can restruc-

All right! Leave me, would you? Have I left something for you!

ture the daily routine with the dog in order to create a less attached relationship. Obviously, if the dog cannot be left in a room on its own when the owner is in the house, there is no chance of leaving it in the house on its own. Significantly more time should be spent with the dog in one room and the owner in another — starting with periods of time which can be counted in seconds, leading up to far longer periods, to the point where the dog can even be shut out of the bedroom at night without it causing a problem.

There must also be a rearrangement of the leaving and returning routine. In general, these dogs either become very depressed when the owner prepares to leave, or become extremely hyperactive and disobedient — some become quite aggressive in an attempt to stop the owner going. The result of this is that the departures become long and drawn-out, because the owner is either trying to cheer up the depressed dog or is physically trying to get out of the door. When the owners return and see the mess, or hear the howling from down the road, they become quite angry with the dog. What we have therefore are warm departures and cool arrivals, as opposed to the routine that automatically develops with the trustworthy dog. Dogs that can be left safely are just told to go to their beds and be good, then off the owner goes to work — cool departure. When they come home, the dog is at the door to greet them and there is an emotional reunion — warm arrival.

The simplest way of achieving this twofold programme is to introduce the dog to the security of an indoor kennel (*see* Appendix for details and instructions on how to do this).

Depending upon the form that the tension-relieving behaviour has taken, we also need to channel the dog's frustrations along suitable lines. It is no good just physically making it impossible for a destructive dog to chew; all that will happen is that you will change the problem to either howling and barking or, worse, self-mutilation. In these cases a more acceptable chew item can be placed inside with the dog. The whole rehabilitation programme should start to show dramatic results within three weeks or so, but some of the more resistant cases can take longer. The first obstacle to overcome is getting the owner to understand that it is his relationship with the dog and the dog's towards him which is causing the problem.

Questions and answers on anxiety-related problems are listed under the alphabetical letter — 'D', destructive behaviour or 'H', house-training, for example.

Babies

The vast majority of dogs quickly accept the arrival of a new human baby into the household without any problems. Most owners give a great deal of thought beforehand to the way the introductions are going to be made and are conscious of the fact they must not create any jealousy between the dog and the baby. I think it is fair to say that most animals recognise the young of another species and, regardless of what that species is, rarely regard it as a threat to themselves. It is this natural phenomenon that allows initial introduction without aggression.

Ideally, the baby should be presented to the dog as soon as it arrives home. This is important because it allows the dog to investigate under controlled conditions. If this is not allowed to happen, the dog's natural curiosity will eventually get the better of him and he will take the first available opportunity to see what all the fuss is about. Dogs that jump up at the side of cots can easily be accused of having evil intentions. The simplest way to do this is to lay the baby on a clean sheet on the floor, bring the dog in on a *loose lead* and allow him to investigate, gently diverting his nose away from the baby's mouth and face. There should be no negative circumstances surrounding this first meeting — no scolding, no smacking, no yanking on the lead; we do not want the dog to learn that the presence of the baby is a prelude to some unpleasant experience. Once his curiosity has been satisfied, he should be given a tit-bit and possibly taken for an enjoyable walk. If this same routine is repeated over the next few meetings, the dog will soon look forward to seeing the baby.

It is a wise new mother who includes the dog in the daily routine with the baby. If the dog is isolated at feeding times, bathing times or nappy-changing times, for example, a resentment can soon build up, especially if prior to the arrival of the baby the dog was allowed total freedom of movement around the house.

It goes without saying that no matter how much you trust your dog with children and babies, they should never be left alone together. Just as jumping up to look into the cot can be misconstrued, so too can dogs investigating dirty nappies.

Question
Why does my dog become such a nuisance whenever I am trying to do anything with the baby? He steals her toys and her clothes if he can get hold of them, but if I shut him out of the room he scratches the door and barks like mad.

Answer
Because he is demanding your attention, which he has learnt that he gets if he runs off with one of her toys — you run after him and tell him off. As you will learn when your baby grows up, dogs, like children, don't care whether the attention is good or bad. The secret is to give him some attention, but only after he has earned it. Start off by going through the routine of bathing the baby, for instance. Put your dog on a lead and secure him to something, tell him to sit and then start to bath the baby. After 30 seconds, provided he has remained quiet and is still sitting, break off and reward the dog. Gentle praise and a juicy tit-bit are a much better reward than being chased around the house by an angry mum. Repeat the procedure but this time don't reward him until a minute of sitting has been completed. You probably won't succeed in giving the baby her bath at the first session, but you will start to teach your dog that obeying a simple command during this daily occurrence will bring reward. Eventually, after he has sat or lain down for a few minutes, you could give him a chew stick to occupy himself with as you finish whatever you are doing.

Bach remedies

Dr Edward Bach (pronounced Batch) was a respected physician, pathologist, immunologist and bacteriologist. In 1919 he accepted a post at the London Homoeopathic hospital. Homoeopathy is a system based on the theory and practice that disease is cured by remedies which produce in a healthy person effects similar to symptoms in the patient.

The remedies are normally administered in minute or even infinitesimal doses, thus minimising the potential for toxic side-effects often found with the use of most allopathic drugs. There are two basic principles involved:

1 That like cures like.
2 That the patient is treated (his or her character), not the disease.

Bach found that this system of healing was very much in line with what he had believed all his life — that most illness is just a physical manifestation of disharmony within the person. He believed that if the person felt positive about himself and what he was doing, that is, had no negative states of mind, then the illness would go away. He knew that homoeopathic remedies achieved this, but felt that they were too difficult for the average person to diagnose and treat themselves. He was convinced that there was a simpler solution that should be available to the lay person and the professional alike.

In 1928, on a visit to Wales, he found, partly through intuition and partly through experimentation, that certain wild flowers had a beneficial effect on people. For instance, Mimulus (*Mimulus guttatus*), when given to a shy or timid person or to someone who had a fear of particular things, overcame this shyness and fear. In 1930, he closed his laboratory and left London to journey through southern England and Wales looking for other naturally occurring substances which would counteract other negative states of mind. By the time he died in 1936 he had discovered thirty-eight remedies which are called the Bach Flower Remedies.

These remedies are easily available, inexpensive and produce no harmful side-effects. What is more important as far as this book is concerned, they work brilliantly on dogs. Although there is no substitute for proper veterinary attention where health is concerned, from a behavioural point of view — where health is not at issue — they are a tremendous asset when dealing with fearful, phobic or aggressive dogs. Providing the referring vet agrees, I have found them a tremendous aid in my work with problem dogs.

Question

I have a three-year-old male Weimaraner who is a show dog. He was doing extremely well until about six months ago when he was attacked in the ring by another dog. Since then he is fine until we get into the ring and then he becomes very apprehensive. Naturally, this shows in the way he carries himself: his tail is tucked in, his head is low and his ears look like they should be on an elephant. We have tried everything to cheer him up but nothing seems to work. At ringcraft classes he is his old self again, so it's not a question of more training. Is there anything that you can suggest?

Answer

Because we are dealing with a situational problem, training is obviously out of the question. Nothing that you can set up will simulate the atmosphere that is found at a real show and your dog will definitely recognise the difference. What is needed is something that will overcome his apprehension within that environment and his fear of a repeat attack. The Bach Flower Remedies are ideal for this sort of problem and a look down the list of remedies available will show you that *Aspen* is for apprehension and vague, unknown fears, *Mimulus* is for fear of known things, *Rock Rose* is for extreme fear, terror and panic. One of these, or a combination of all three, might do the trick. Ideally, you should ask your vet to refer you to a homoeopathic vet who will prescribe the right remedies to suit your particular dog, but don't worry, they will bounce your dog back into the show ring with the right attitude again.

Barking

In Part Two we established that dogs bark; it is a perfectly normal thing for them to do when they want to give warning and call for assistance. Persistent barking, however, can drive owners and neighbours up the wall. Some breeds are naturally more vociferous than others, so if you are looking for a relatively quiet dog, don't buy one of the guarding breeds. If you do have a guarding breed, don't give it the run of your garden when you go to work, otherwise you will come home to find some irate neighbours brandishing a court order. Having accepted that the basic function of barking is to give warning, a lot of dogs bark for other reasons.

They bark as an attention-seeking behaviour; they bark out

of excitement; some highly excitable types bark at every little noise, and some dogs bark for the sheer hell of it. If you have a problem barker, it is sensible to try and establish what triggers it off and whether this is the area that you should be controlling. Finally, you should ask yourself the question: Is it the barking that I find a problem or the fact that he won't stop when I tell him? If it is the latter, then the problem is one of control, not barking.

Invariably, the owners resort to trying to outshout the dog in their attempts to shut it up. As far as the dog is concerned, it is pleased that its owners are joining in and so the problem gets worse, not better. I have found that the most effective way of dealing with a noisy dog is to use sound to combat sound (*see* Appendix for the application of sound aversion therapy). Naturally, all other factors should be considered before you look at ways of controlling a problem — such as diet-related excitability, attention-seeking and other possible causative factors.

Question
I have a lovely rescue Samoyed bitch of 14 months called Sammy. She obviously has had no previous training but is responding very well to everything that I am teaching her, but she has one annoying habit that I can't seem to break. We have a very large garden (two acres) in which there stands a large beech tree. For years this has been the home for squirrels. Every morning, when I let Sammy out into the garden, she rushes straight to this tree and barks furiously at the squirrels. This doesn't appear to bother them one bit, but I am sure my neighbours are not very happy about it. The problem is that the tree is too far away from the house for me to scold her properly — she will do as she is told when she is close to me, but she seems to know that once I am a certain distance away, there is nothing I can do to stop her.

Answer
Then don't try to stop her, get the squirrels to do it for you — or at least get Sammy to think that it is the squirrels.

The big problem here is that the whole business is self-rewarding as far as Sammy is concerned. There is the fun of the chase and the frustration of the squirrels just sitting there — out of reach and refusing to move any more. What we need to do is to take the fun out of it for her but, because of the distance from the tree to the house, any correction coming from the house will be ineffective as you have already found. Therefore, the correction has to come from the tree itself, or better still the squirrels.

Get a hosepipe that is long enough to stretch from the tap to the tree and, with a ladder, position the end of it in the branches, pointing down to where Sammy usually puts her brakes on. Just before you let her out, make sure that the hose is full of water so that there will be no delay when you turn on the tap. As soon as she opens her mouth to start barking, let her have a short, sharp squirt. Don't leave it running because she will just avoid it and move round the other side. If she is clever enough to learn that there is only one place where the squirrels retaliate, you will have to keep re-positioning the hose to fire from different angles each time. Don't say a word to her yourself; this is between her, the tree and the squirrels. Water is an extremely effective, harmless shock tactic and if your timing is good, she won't want to go near the tree again.

Biting

Dogs start learning to bite from a very early age. One of the reasons why mother nature gives puppies stupid little useless needles for teeth is so that when they are play-fighting with their little brothers and sisters and they bite too hard, they hurt — that's the only reason why they have them, to cause pain. It is important that, from as early an age as possible, dogs learn how to control their jaw muscles and learn what is called 'bite inhibition'. Between about four and eighteen weeks, their jaw muscles are not properly developed and so those sharp little teeth are there as a substitute for the lack of power. It is perfectly normal therefore for our puppies to bite us; they are undergoing a natural learning process and it is our job to teach them, at this stage, that biting humans is not acceptable.

The usual owner-response to a puppy that has just sunk its lethal little fangs into us is to shout 'NO' and tap it on the nose or smack its bum. This is a very confusing reaction as far as the puppy is concerned and, if it has any learning value at all, it would be that when you bite a human you have to dart away quickly — not that you don't bite in the first place. The best way to teach them not to bite is to observe what happens between two puppies. When one bites too hard the other yelps and the biter lets go immediately. If we let out a sharp cry of pain every time our puppy's teeth come into contact with our skin (don't wait until it hurts), we can very quickly desensitise it altogether to using its teeth on us. Contrary to popular opinion, we are not teaching it that it can easily hurt us because the learning phase that they are going through is about how to use their teeth properly. Using them for dominant purposes does not arise until the adult teeth come through.

It should be obvious, therefore, that this bite inhibition towards humans must be taught before about eighteen weeks. It is around this time that the puppy teeth start to fall out and the adult teeth are pushing through. Once this stage is entered, there should be no contact at all between the puppy's teeth and your skin or clothing. Regardless of how gently it grasps your hand in its mouth, it is done for one reason only and that is to dominate you. Usually a very sudden, very loud 'GET OFF', combined with piercing eye contact, will teach it that you are not amused by its behaviour, especially if you ignore it for a minute or so afterwards. Whatever you do, do not say 'there's a good dog' when it lets go. There should be absolutely no rewarding circumstances during any stage of an interaction between you which involves the puppy's teeth.

Question
We have a two-year old Border Collie dog called Ben which is forever biting me and the rest of the family on the ankles. He never hurts us and he doesn't ever become aggressive, but we just can't seem to stop him. Someone suggested hitting him with a rolled-up newspaper, but the big problem is that we never know when he is going to do it so we are never prepared. Can you suggest something?

Answer
What he is doing is herding you all, which I am sure you will have realised. A quick nip on the ankles is the quickest way of making you move a bit faster, and even if you all walked around armed with rolled-up newspapers, he would just learn to nip and duck. The Border Collie at work is always very aware that the animal that it is herding is capable of retaliating, but that doesn't stop it herding.

I would be surprised if the behaviour could not be predicted. I think that the mistake you are making in trying to work out when he is likely to do it is that you are only looking at what the bitee is doing at the time. You need to look at what the rest of the family is doing as well and I think you will almost certainly find that it is either when they are all in one room and someone gets up to leave, or when the family is scattered around the house. Ben will have some sense of order in how you should all be contained. For you to establish what he considers to be neat and orderly, you have to view the entire household. Once you can predict the circumstances, you are then in a position to interrupt the bite. I would use sound aversion therapy (*see* Appendix) to teach him that his actions create unpleasant reactions. Although we are talking about an inherent instinct within this breed, what is interesting about it is that no matter how quickly he approaches, the bite is totally controlled — just enough to make you move and not enough to cause any pain or damage. As you say, he is not aggressive. NB. Herding instincts will be discussed again under 'H', p. 135.

Boarding

There is always one very important rule to remember when you are considering putting your dog into a boarding establishment; LOOK BEFORE YOU BOOK. If you don't like what you see, don't expect that it will improve by the time your dog arrives. All boarding establishments for animals must be licensed by the local authority, but having a licence is not an indication of quality. The standards laid down by each individual authority are always minimum standards, and as long as the kennels adhere to the minimum, they are granted a licence.

Unfortunately, in many cases, the minimum is not fit to keep any animal in, let alone a dog that has probably spent all of its previous existence having its every whim being pandered to in the comfort of a modern home. There is a boarding kennels near my home, and over the years I have heard so many detrimental comments from dog and cat owners about the place that I contacted the local authority and asked them why they continued to grant a licence. Their reply was: '*Providing they supply the minimum facilities laid down by the regulations, like heating and exercise facilities, for example, a licence will be granted. The fact that we cannot enforce whether the heating is ever turned on or the animals are allowed access to the exercise areas is a sad fact of life. If we denied them the licence, it would mean that hundreds of people per year would have nowhere to board their pets locally.*' Well, how sad! If the owner is planning to jet off to an exotic location a few thousand miles away, why shouldn't he be prepared to travel 40 or 50 miles to ensure that his dog is going to be looked after properly?

Vets in general will not recommend a boarding establishment. They will supply you with a list and they will allow kennels to advertise on their notice-board, but if you ask your vet to recommend one and your dog comes back looking ill for any reason, the owner is going to blame the vet. So not being recommended by the vet is not to be construed as the opposite, it is purely to cover themselves. The best way to find the right place is through personal recommendation and your own gut reaction.

Question
I am planning to put my dog into a boarding kennel for the first time next month. I have heard nothing but good reports about the place and I have been to see it myself and was very impressed. The problem is that my dog is very attached to me and I am not sure how he will cope — I just know that the worry about how he will be feeling is going to spoil my holiday. Can you give me any advice that will help him to settle in quicker?

Answer
Most dogs adapt very quickly to different environments — usually in about two days. Therefore it might upset you to hear that all the time that you are pining for him, providing he is well fed, warm and feels secure, he will not be pining for you. It is my experience that dogs that arrive for boarding with a whole host of chemical reminders of their home (blankets, beds, toys, old slippers) tend to cling to these familiar objects and take longer to adjust to their new surroundings than dogs which arrive without them. Provided you are happy that you have booked him into the right place, go and enjoy your holiday. Don't over-compensate for your guilt before you go and don't apologise when you come home. (*See also* Anorexia nervosa (question), p. 73; Anthropomorphism (question), p. 75.)

Bones
I think that most pet owners have the impression that dogs need bones. Provided their diet is adequate, they do not. For sure, most dogs like a good marrow bone to chew on, and if this is the case and everyone can approach the dog while it is eating one, by all means give it a bone. It should go without saying

that bones that can splinter should be avoided, so chicken bones and the like are out. The other popular reason for giving dogs bones is to help them clean their teeth. Once again, a balanced diet will do the job just as well and there are doggy toothpastes available if your dog's teeth build up plaque — your vet will advise you on this.

In short, contrary to popular opinion, bones are not an essential part of a dog's diet. Perhaps they used to be in the days when the dog had to make do with the left-over scraps, but with the modern range of commercial dog foods available today they are surplus to requirements and, in some cases, can cause more harm than good. In warm weather they are a magnet for flies' eggs, and we all tend to leave the dog with the bone for too long. Also, in multi-dog environments, the bone can become something to trophy between them and might become the catalyst for fights, even in the most friendly pack situation.

Question

I have a perfectly friendly Golden Retriever dog of 15 months, except when I recently gave him a bone. He took it straight into his bed and nobody could go near him — the change that came over him was frightening. The only way we could get it off him was by someone knocking on the door, and when he ran to the door we took the bone away. Even then, for the rest of the day he was extremely aggressive when anyone went near his bed. What should I do about it?

Answer

Don't give him any more bones. He doesn't need them and what you have witnessed is not uncommon with some dogs and bones. To the dog, bones are food, but it is food that cannot be eaten straight away and therefore the dog instinctively needs to let everyone know that he intends to keep it — unlike his daily food ration which can be eaten in one go and usually is. There is also the question of palatability: in general a fresh marrow bone is infinitely more palatable than commercial dog food and this increases the food-guarding instinct and primitive reaction that drove your dog to its bed with the bone. First of all, it was portable food — unlike his food bowl. Next, he knew it was a long-term food source and therefore needed to be taken to a safe haven — possibly with the intention of burying it. It was for this reason that he continued to protect the area after the bone had been removed; he probably thought he had hidden it there.

If a bone can trigger off a primitive reaction in your dog, to the point that he might become dangerous, don't allow the issue to be raised again. It would be a wise move, however, to consider two areas that might be contributing towards this sudden and out-of-character behaviour, just in case he gets access to a bone in the future.

1   Is he getting the right nutritional requirements? A dog that is nutritionally satisfied does not need to trophy additional food so vigorously.
2   Are you satisfied with how your dog sees his role within your mixed canine/human pack? If he regards himself as pretty high-ranking, then he is going to consider that he has a perfect right to guard food from the rest of the pack.

Cars

A great many of my canine clients announce their arrival long before their owners drive them into my car park. I can hear them coming across the common that is alongside where I live — squealing and barking because they have seen some open land, or another dog, or a person, or a bike, or have heard the indicator flashing, or just because the car is moving. They usually arrive in a state of exhaustion, with the owners looking stressed and weary.

Why is it that cars seem to excite dogs so much? Simply because they have become a prelude to an exciting occasion. As I mentioned in Chapter 3, most families now have a second car, usually a hatchback or an estate to carry the dog. The dog is driven to the park, probably on a daily or twice-daily basis. He is isolated in the back and allowed to jump from side to side because he is not jumping all over people. We have a situation, therefore, where getting in the car means heading for the park and no control is exercised over his behaviour during the journey. This regular scenario is guaranteed to produce an 'over-the-top', car-crazy traveller. It is an interesting fact that very few dogs become car-crazy if the family only have a saloon model, simply because it is not practical and highly dangerous to allow the dog to jump from seat to seat. Dogs that do start to develop this tendency are quickly stopped by being tethered whilst the car is moving.

There are various techniques that can be employed to calm a crazy traveller. Tethering him in the back is usually the most effective. Just because you have a car that has ample room for the dog does not mean the dog has to use it all. A lead about three feet long (sorry, a metre) secured at one end and attached to an ordinary leather buckle collar — definitely not a choke collar — is all that is required. This allows the dog to lie down, stand up and turn round, but it stops him from charging from side to side. It also means that you have effective control when opening the tailgate.

If this does not produce the desired calming effect, then sound aversion therapy (*see* Appendix) may be required to interrupt the learned behaviour. For the really persistent offenders, tethering them below window level can prove useful, or obtaining a car travel cage and draping a sheet over it to block their view, movement being a prime motivator with some dogs.

If it can be arranged, the car is not used for a fortnight or so to take the dog for exercise. Put him in there to go shopping or for local trips, but do r.ot get him out again until you get home. What you are doing is changing his expectations about what getting in the car means — instead of arriving at the park, he keeps arriving back home.

Question
I have a six-month-old Yorkshire Terrier called Jenny who is absolutely terrified of travelling in the car; she whimpers and shakes the whole time, even when it's not moving. I try to reassure her but it doesn't seem to make much difference. She used to be sick within minutes of setting off, but that seems to be getting better now. Is there anything I can do to get her used to travelling?

Answer
Perseverance is the best advice that I can give. The fact that her car sickness is getting better is an indication that she is getting used to the strange movement. Reassuring her when she is whimpering might in fact be making the problem worse. If you think about it, you are rewarding the behaviour that you do not want. Gentle words and soft caresses are just sounds and strokes to a dog, exactly what she would experience if you told her to sit and she did. The behaviour that you do want is for her to remain quiet, but I bet you don't stroke her then for fear of disturbing her.

The secret, then, is to make sure that you are rewarding the right behaviour, and to keep all your journeys short with very rewarding experiences at the end of them — a run in the park, or her food. It will also pay dividends for you to feed her in the car without it being moved at all.

Castration

A tremendous amount of 'old wives' tales' are attached to this relatively simple operation. Dogs get fat; they lose their character; poor dog, it's not fair on him, how would you like it? — and many more. For sure, they might get fat if you let them, simply because they generally become more relaxed and therefore don't metabolise at the rate that they used to, so they don't need as much food. They don't *lose* their character, it generally improves, so it would be partly true to say that it changes their character, but only for the better; what that means is that it never makes a dog worse. As for the poor dog pining over his testicles, that is complete anthropomorphism.

Research conducted in America at the University of Pennsylvania in 1970 showed a better than 70 per cent improvement in the behaviour of dogs that were castrated, regardless of their age. This lays another 'old wives' tale' to rest, that it won't make any difference once the dog is over two years old. Improvement was noted in dogs that were castrated when they were twelve years old.

These findings were borne out in this country in 1988, when one of my students on the correspondence course that I was commissioned to write for the Canine Studies Institute, Hazel Palmer (now an associate member of the APBC and an assistant in my practice), submitted a survey that she had completed on the effects of surgical castration on problem behaviour in adult dogs. Her results showed a slightly higher success rate than did the American survey, but both of them clearly gave the message that there is a very high chance of improved behaviour.

Some vets are very much against castrating dogs to improve their behaviour, stating that it is 'social surgery' — an operation carried out for the convenience of the owners. That might be so in some cases, but if more dogs not used for breeding purposes were castrated, there would not be so many stray and unwanted dogs around.

I wholeheartedly agree with my APBC colleague John Rogerson, when he states that, in his opinion, leaving a male dog entire, with all the natural urges that this produces, and then denying him any outlet for these urges for the rest of his life, is cruel.

Question
I have a twelve-month-old Dobermann which is becoming more and more aggressive towards other dogs. It's only males; females he loves. Is it just that he is an adolescent and will grow out of it, or should I have him castrated?

Answer
There may be an element of adolescent behaviour involved. At this age there is quite a rise in the testosterone level (male hormone) which won't settle down properly until he is about eighteen months old. The danger is that by that time his behaviour might have become learned.

There are certain clues which will help you to establish whether the problem is hormone-related. The first clue is already there — he hates males and loves females. Does he also sniff and drool a lot when he is out? Does he frequently mark territory, usually the same places? Does he scratch the ground after marking, possibly with raised hackles and growling as he does it? Does he exhibit anti-social sexual behaviour (like attempting intercourse with the vicar's leg when he comes round for tea)? If the answer to these questions is yes, then I think you should discuss with your vet the possibility of having him castrated. You may be advised to try a short-term anti-androgenic course of treatment (so-called chemical castration). This can prove effective in some cases but does not always work. If it does, it will show you what your dog will be like after castration and might persuade you to go ahead if you are uncertain. My personal opinion is that if you have no problem about having your dog castrated, then why mess about with hormone treatment when we really don't know what the long-term effects will be? We don't hesitate to castrate tom cats, horses, pigs and bullocks, so why do we have this psychological problem over dogs? Could it be another indication of the close bond between us?

Cats
Most cartoons depicting dogs and cats will show the dog chasing the cat, which is usually the case. Why do dogs chase cats? Because cats run, it's as simple as that. Cat-chasing is good sport for a dog and rarely is there any predatory intent involved. In the rare event of the dog cornering the cat, the dog hasn't got a clue what to do next. If he gets striped across the

nose by the cat's claws (which incidentally can operate seven times faster than the dog can operate its jaws), then invariably the dog will back off and allow the cat to escape.

Most dogs learn to live side-by-side with a cat in the same house. This happens in thousands of homes up and down the country and really dispels any idea that the dog and the cat are mortal enemies. My own dogs live quite amiably with two cats, even though our rescued Jack Russell was reported to be a cat killer when we got her at fifteen months old. But if they see each other in the garden, the chase is on. The cats always escape and I sometimes wonder whether there is as much fun in it for them as there is for the dogs.

Question

I have a two-year-old rescued Boxer dog called Tyson. We have had him about two weeks and he is really settling in well. The problem is that our five-year-old cat will not accept him and has chosen to live outside. She only comes in to eat and as soon as she has finished she goes out again. How can I get them both to accept each other?

Answer

You don't say what the dog's attitude is to the cat, so I can only assume that he is not aggressive towards her, otherwise you would have mentioned it — he obviously just frightens her.

I think that your long-standing resident — the cat — feels that her territory has been violated by another animal. She obviously still feels tied to this territory because she returns to it to eat, but if you do not do something quickly, that might change.

Cats live where it suits them best and if she is spending more time round at a neighbour's because of Tyson, the chances are that your neighbour will become attached to her, start feeding her and she will re-locate. It is a sad fact of life that we do not own cats — cats own territory.

You need to re-establish her rights over her territory. The best way to do this is one room at a time. The next time she comes in to eat, put her into a fairly spacious cage, one that is big enough to contain a litter tray, water and feed bowl, as well as giving her a separate sleeping area. Any unwelcome attention by Tyson should be interrupted by one of the aversion therapy methods mentioned in the Appendix to this book, except the screech alarm which might affect the cat. What you are trying to do is establish your cat's right to occupy each room in turn, without giving either animal the chance to initiate a game of chase. Tyson, as the newcomer, should learn that certain actions create reactions — that is, the cat is not for chasing.

It will take two or three days to re-establish residency in each room frequented by both animals, but the end result will be worth the effort. Where cats are concerned you have to make the decisions, otherwise they will make their own.

Chase

Following on nicely from the previous subject, all dog owners know how highly developed the chase instinct is in their dogs — some breeds more than others. There are two basic ingredients that need to be determined prior to making any decision about how the chase problem is going to be corrected.

1 Is it chasing for the fun of chasing?
2 Is there a predatory involvement — that is, a killing intent?

If it is for the sheer fun of chasing, we need to redirect the fun to a more acceptable pastime. For example, if it likes chasing balls but the problem behaviour is chasing joggers, we need to take the fun out of chasing joggers and replace it with a ball-chasing game.

If the chase problem has a predatory intent, there are other criteria which should be considered first.

1 Can the chase victim be avoided at all times (in the case of sheep)?
2 Can increased control and training overcome the problem if it cannot be avoided?
3 Are you prepared to take the aversion therapy to its ultimate or are you prepared to consider euthanasia?

Fun chasers usually have a favourite toy which they love you to throw for them. By taking possession of that toy (and all other toys so that they do not just choose something else) and only playing games with it when on a walk, especially when a jogger comes into sight, you are satisfying the chase instinct in the area where it has become a problem — away from home. If you think about it, at home its chasing games are played whenever it wants to play them because the toys are there all the time. When on a walk, there are usually no toys but there are joggers and the times that it can play chase with them is limited. By restricting all ball-chase games to walks only and interrupting any tendency to chase other things (*see* Appendix, sound aversion therapy) you can quickly redirect the problem. The sound aversion works better if you can solicit the help of a friend to play the part of the jogger and get him or her to control the sound.

My APBC colleague John Rogerson describes the importance of toys in his two books: *Your Dog, Its Development, Behaviour and Training* and *Understanding Your Dog*.

Predatory chasers can often be cured by similar sound aversion methods, but in these cases I recommend that the chase instinct is not encouraged at all. These dogs do not see the ball as something to be chased, they see it as something to be brought down and killed. The way that they pounce upon, shake and stand over anything that you care to throw for them will show you the difference in attitude between them and the whoopee chasers. This is an instinct that has to be discouraged at all costs. If this is a problem with your dog, what you should ask yourself is this : 'If I threw a ball for my dog, could I stop it running after it when it was half-way there?'

If the answer is no, then you would not stop it from chasing sheep. Again, we need to redirect the behaviour, but this time the reward is for not running. The predatorial instinct is food-related, therefore food becomes the reward — initially, part of its daily food ration, and later tit-bits, providing they are not overused. The dog should be on an extending leash so that, if necessary, you can physically deny it the reward of the chase. As soon as the dog sets off after the thrown ball, the aversion is sounded. It is called back to you and rewarded. This procedure is kept up until the dog returns of its own free will when it hears the aversive sound. Eventually, the dog should come to you whenever anything is thrown rather than go after the object. Believe it or not, this can be achieved fairly quickly with one article (say a ball) in one particular area. The next stage is to change the area and achieve the same result. Then do it in another area until the dog understands the principle that if something moves fast, chasing it is unpleasant, not chasing it is rewarding.

This principle must be established without question on balls, sticks, bikes, cars and anything else, before the dog is exposed to sheep again. This time you will need to be accompanied by someone who is also going to operate whatever aversive technique you have found successful — the object being to double the aversion. Although in general, sound aversion techniques are used to make a particular action unpleasant, with predatory sheep chasers we need to make the dog frightened of chasing them. If you have managed to control the chase instinct in general, this increased reaction in the presence of sheep should do the trick. There is a school of thought that using the technique for fun chasing will have the same effect on predatory chasers. That might well be so, but in these cases I prefer to transfer the whole behaviour off chasing anything, onto food.

Many people believe 'the old wives' tale' that the way to stop sheep chasers is to tie the dog up in a shed with a ram. First you need someone with a co-operative ram, usually a farmer who will have a much better way of stopping your dog from chasing his sheep — it's called a shotgun.

No doubt rams have been used successfully in the past, but we never hear of the number of times it hasn't worked; we never hear about the rams and dogs that have been seriously injured, and anyway, the ram will only attack because it can't run away (a fear response). Where dogs and sheep are concerned, whether your dog is predatorial or not, the safest thing is to avoid taking or allowing your dog near them. It's not always what the dog does to the sheep that causes the damage, it can be what the sheep does to itself through the sheer panic of seeing a running dog. Frightened sheep will run into fences, ditches and bogs, and farmers can suffer a great deal of financial loss through sheep aborting their lambs because they have been chased by a dog. If the farmer doesn't shoot the dog, the courts may order it to be destroyed.

Question
I have a three-year-old Bearded Collie dog which is terrible at chasing cars that go up and down our lane, and biting their tyres. He lies there waiting for them all day. Up to now he has never been hurt but I am sure that one day he will be. He doesn't bother with cars anywhere else. Why does he do it, and how can I stop him?

Answer
It's a combination of an accelerated chase instinct and an over-protection of property — Beardies are renowned for chasing cars, trains, in fact anything that moves fast and makes a noise. Presumably, he has freedom of access to the lane, which probably means that because he is allowed this sort of freedom, he does not get much off-territory exercise. If this is the case, he must be given more stimulative exercise and this in itself will reduce the need to stimulate himself through the work that *he thinks* he is doing. Denying him access to the lane would be the easiest way of stopping the problem, but again, he must be taken off-territory regularly to compensate for this loss of freedom. At the end of the day, a simple form of aversion might work, like getting someone to drive slowly past with a passenger, an open window and a bucket of water. As soon as the dog gets in range, let him have the lot. Two or three repetitions should stop him chasing cars, but unless you satisfy his working instincts, he will only transfer his territorial chase behaviour elsewhere.

Chewing
Dogs chew for a variety of reasons. When they are teething is the first obvious reason which most of us understand and, to a certain extent, accept. Not many people, however, are aware that some dogs can go through another teething period when the adult teeth are settling into the jaw bone (between six and twelve months). With some dogs this can cause a great deal of discomfort and there is a physiological need to chew. Incorrect diets can create chewing problems, especially if there is fibre deficiency in the food — door frames, table legs, tissues and toilet rolls then become a sensible source of fibre as far as the dog is concerned. Lack of exercise and mental stimulation can create a major cause of chewing — boredom. A bored dog that is left on its own all day will eventually stumble across mum's new shoes; they have a nice smell of new leather, as well as of mum, so they are licked and nibbled, partly as a comforter, usually through play. The more they are licked and nibbled, the softer and more pliable they become, and a wonderful new toy to chew on. The whole act of chewing becomes self-rewarding. Sometimes, one is ripped in an attempt to flatten it so that the dog can lie on it as a chemical reminder of mum until she returns. These actions are not done out of spite or with any

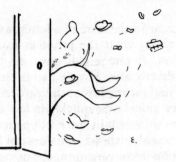

A destructive dog is often a bored dog.

attempt to destroy valuable property on purpose — like the wolf, dogs have no sense of values. Throughout the time they are involved in their chewing, they are being rewarded. It comes as a great confusing shock to them, therefore, that when they rush to the door to greet whoever is returning, that person is annoyed and often aggressive. This confusion accounts for one of the other causes of chewing — Anxiety (*see* p. 76).

Before correcting a problem chewer, as with all other problems, the root cause has to be established: age in relation to dental development; activity level in relation to exercise; over-attachment to owner, which will encourage the need to be close to something that contains the person's scent in their absence; whether the chewing is fibre-based and possibly diet-related; whether it is anxiety-related. Having decided the cause, the information in the Appendix (indoor kennels), under Diet (p. 32 and p. 106) or Anxiety (p. 76) will help you to formulate a cure.

Question
My two-year-old Boxer bitch Flossie has suddenly started chewing everything she can get her teeth into. In fact she doesn't just chew, she shreds. To date she has destroyed numerous newspapers, two cushions, a doormat, and an area of carpet — although I think she did that with her claws because she has also started digging holes in the garden. We have never had any trouble with her in the past, not even when she was a puppy.

Answer

This question came in the form of a letter, and although I had my suspicions about what the problem was, I needed some more information. A phone call gave me the answers. The problem arose shortly after Flossie had been in season, during which time she had escaped from the garden but was found by a neighbour very quickly. So quickly in fact that they were not worried that anything could have happened to her. Wrong! Obviously, the neighbourhood stud does not hang around. Following our telephone conversation, the owners took her to the vet and he confirmed that Flossie was pregnant. The clues were in the fact that her chewing activity was noticeably to shred things and the fact that she had started to dig — both in the house and garden — also, that her behaviour was sudden in onset and was completely out of character. Her owners saw the behaviour as chewing, Flossie saw it as nesting. The owners decided to let her have the pups (a decision on which I reserve judgement), and by providing her with a whelping box and blankets effectively stopped the chewing.

Children

There is no doubt that the behaviour of a dog is greatly influenced by the behaviour of the children within the household in which it lives. This is especially true when the dog has been raised in that environment since it was a puppy. A calm environment will have a calming influence on the pup, and vice-versa. I see many dogs that are reported to be hyperactive by their owners. Because I generally like to see the dog with the whole family, these so-called hyperactive dogs are usually accompanied by so-called hyperactive children.

I accept the fact that some children are genuinely hyperactive, and I am one of the first to suspect additives, preservatives and other chemicals as a contributory cause of some hyperactivity, but I think that we are giving parents and dog owners a wonderful 'cop-out' excuse for lack of general control. Two questions arise: are there far more hyperactive children around, and subsequently far more hyperactive dogs, than there used to be? If so, is this hyperactivity a direct result of more permissive parents who want to allow their children to express themselves, or is the greater influence the type of food, television, or changes in teaching attitudes? It would be an interesting experiment if all parents in the country changed their children's diet for a week and reported the results. Those who achieved beneficial results could examine the diet in more depth; those who did not could start to look at their children's life-style. Cloud-cuckoo-land, I know, but it would start to lay the blame on the right doorstep and, as a knock-on effect, it would improve the behaviour of a lot of dogs.

What I am saying is that some children are not good for dogs, especially where the dog's behaviour is concerned. My experience is that parents who can control their children generally have more manageable dogs. But I firmly believe that dogs are good for children in many ways. The dog becomes a companion and something that the children can talk to and confide in. The dog never breaks this confidence and never offers an opinion back. Dogs give children a sense of security and, quite often, a sense of responsibility. Dogs teach children to handle bereavement because of their much shorter life-span. There is no doubt in my mind that the benefits for children who live with dogs far outweigh the disadvantages.

The problems really arise with dogs which are not confident around children. For childless couples who buy a puppy, early exposure to children under controlled circumstances is a must if future problems are to be avoided. Where this has not happened, the erratic movements and high-pitched voices of children have an unsettling effect on the dog. Most dogs can be desensitised (*see* Desensitise, p. 105) to this by taking control of the children and slowing them down.

Making sure that the dog receives no tit-bits at all for a period of a few weeks, unless they are given by a child, will quickly change most dog's expectations about what the presence of children really means. This, of course, will only be done where the exposure to children cannot be avoided; to be safe, if you do not trust your dog with children, do not take the risk.

Question

I have two dogs: an eighteen-month-old male German Shepherd Dog and a two-year-old female Rottweiler. We live on a corner plot with a reasonably large garden. It is well fenced with six-foot high close-lapped boarding, but the problem is that it is near a school and every school morning the children tease the dogs by banging on the fence and sometimes throwing things over. It drives my dogs wild to the point where I have to keep them in. Even then, the dogs can still hear the banging and bark furiously in the house. I am frightened that if the dogs get near to one of these children, they will bite. This would be tragic because they are both usually of good temperament. Is there anything that I can do about it?

Answer
You are right to be frightened. I think that under the circumstances a bite situation is a very real danger. What these children are doing, without realising it, is conditioning your dogs to something called 'Freedom Reflex Biting'. Any animal that is contained or tethered and exposed regularly to an annoying stimulus will eventually, if given the opportunity, attack that stimulus. Your particular problem is further complicated because you have two dogs of the guarding breeds. Short of moving house, your wisest move is to keep the dogs indoors as you are doing. Perhaps some sound aversion therapy (*see* Appendix) will interrupt their barking indoors, but the only effective solution is to take away the stimulus.

In your situation, I would visit the school and explain to the headteacher just what the potential risk is. If your dogs are good-natured, it might be a good idea to take them, too (with prior agreement, of course).

Suggest to the teacher that it would be sensible for the local dog warden to visit the school and talk to all the children about dogs in general, but nicely slipping in the danger of annoying dogs that are behind some form of barrier. This can be done without accusing anyone of anything in particular — after all, what the children are doing is great fun to them, they just do not understand the consequences.

Choke chains
Throughout this book, I refer to the use of the choke chain. Before any of the readers think it, I know that they are now called check chains because that is what they are designed to do — check, not choke. When they first came into this country from Germany, around the time of the First World War, they were called choke chains, and a writer in one of the dog papers at the time called them cruel and barbaric. They continued to be called choke chains for many years, and even the Home Office manual on training police dogs referred to them as this until very recently. Just when they started to be known as check chains I do not know, but although it sounds a kinder piece of

equipment, in the hands of a novice it still performs the same function — it chokes. My argument against them is that they are freely available in most pet shops, with no advice on how to put one on properly, no advice on how to use one, no advice on how to measure the dog for one and no consideration about whether the dog is touch-sensitive or not (*see* Sensitivity, p. 190). My other objection is that I see far too many dogs that arrive at my premises dragging their owners along behind them. These dogs invariably have bulging red eyes and blue tongues because their blood and air supply are being restricted through the tightness of the chain, yet still they pull. Quite often there is evidence of muscle and tissue damage to the dog's neck, caused by the constant pressure of the chain. In every case the owners state that they got the chain to stop the dog pulling.

My final objection is that I have not had cause to use one for many years, thus proving that they are not necessary. The only reason why they are used so much by pet owners is that we have all come to accept the choke as the standard anti-pulling equipment, without giving it any real thought (*see* Pulling, p. 167, for alternatives).

Compulsion

It is a sad fact of life that the way dogs have been trained for many years has been with the attitude 'You dog, me man, I say, you will', and when they don't, we have forced them. The dictionary definition of compulsion is: *irresistible urge to form a behaviour against one's normal wishes*. That doesn't conjure up a picture in my mind of man and dog working in harmony, which is surely everyone's idea of our relationship. It is an interesting fact that we do not train other animals with compulsion, nor do we ourselves learn through compulsion. We may perform a particular activity against our wishes if we are forced to do so, but what we learn is to avoid the enforcer. Surely, we are in great danger of teaching our dogs to do the same if we use this training principle. Would it not be better to encourage a dog to do something for reward, so teaching it to do it because it likes to (*see* Reinforcement, p. 179).

Question
I have been attending training classes for some time now, and still I can't get my dog to lie down when he is told. I have tried

all the methods suggested — pushing him just behind the shoulder blades whilst pulling his neck down with the lead and choke chain, stepping on the lead and pulling up in order to pull the dog down from the neck; all we ever manage to do is to get into a tussle. If I do succeed in getting him down, I have to hold him there because as soon as I let go, he gets up again. We have reached the point where if I say 'down' he runs off if he can, or goes very rigid if he is on the lead. Can you offer any suggestions, please?

Answer
You have actually taught your dog that the word 'down' is a prelude to an unpleasant experience. It is a normal reaction with any animal, including humans, that as soon as pressure is applied in one direction, it is resisted in the opposite direction. It is called by the lovely scientific term of Negative Thigmotaxis (pressure invites counter-pressure). If you think about it from the dog's point of view, when it first heard the word 'down' and, having absolutely no concept of what it meant, was then forced to the floor, it would automatically resist. This resistance would produce more pressure and a struggle would begin. What he learned was that the word 'down' meant 'push up'.

When we are training dogs, the priority is to teach them what we mean by each particular sound. If we are going to use methods that produce resistance, the learning process is going to be obstructed because they are concentrating on resisting, instead of concentrating on learning. I suggest that you change the command to 'flat', a word that he is not frightened of. Offer him a tit-bit under a low coffee table or similar obstruction so that he has to lie down to reach it. As he does so, tell him 'flat' and give him the tit-bit. After a few repetitions, he will understand what he must do to get the reward and then the coffee table can be discarded. This exercise can be repeated three or four times throughout the day without the dog getting bored. It is very simple, very effective and totally pressureless.

D

Den
See Appendix, Indoor Kennels.

Desensitise
This is a term that is used quite often by behaviourists to describe the process of getting a dog to accept something which previously it could not, by lowering the dog's sensitivity or fear. A dog that is frightened of a particular loud noise, for example, can be desensitised by playing a recording of that noise very quietly whilst preparing the dog's food, progressing to playing it when the dog is eating. Playing the noise, at a very low volume, prior to any enjoyable activity, soon starts to reduce the dog's fear and replaces it with happy anticipation. The volume can be gradually increased, all the time being mindful of the dog's reaction. This technique really involves controlled and gradual exposure to some fearful stimulus, using a reward-based routine for passive acceptance. It can be achieved quickly in some cases, or may take a long time in others, but it should never be rushed. Any sudden escalation of the programme can negate all the good that might have been done up to that point. I have included this brief explanation because this technique is advised in some of the answers to the questions.

Destructiveness

Question
Why does my dog become so destructive when we leave him? He is a three-year-old mongrel called Ben, and up until six months ago he was no problem. Then my husband had to go away on business for three weeks, and Ben was very grumbly with him when he returned. The problem arose after this time.

Answer

Because he objects to being left, is the short answer. While your husband was away, Ben took over the role of Alpha male. You might have had a hand in promoting him to this rank without realising it — perhaps you let the dog sleep in your bedroom for company during those three weeks.

If so, it is no wonder Ben was grumbly when your husband came home. A three-week period of greater attention and increased privileges is more than sufficient time for a dog to get a different idea of his role within your environment. Ben needs demoting quickly, not just so that you have the right to contain him, but for the safety of your husband. If it is Ben's opinion that in your husband's absence he is in charge, when he returns there will be a challenge for that position. However, if Ben sees that in your husband's absence you are in charge, there will be no problem when he comes back, regardless of how long he has been away.

As far as the destructiveness is concerned, isolating a dog that has a high regard for his rank is rather like the office junior saying to the managing director, 'Just pop in to that room and wait for me, I will be along to talk to you shortly.' There is no way that a higher ranking human is going to wait in a room on the instructions, and for the convenience, of a lower rank. On the other hand, if the managing director gave that sort of instruction, he would expect to be obeyed without question. Whether you want to be the managing director or your husband does makes no difference, so long as Ben accepts that he is the office junior. This is a form of anxiety, but not one that is attachment-related. Chapter 3 will give you some ways of overcoming the problem. (*See also* Chewing, p. 98.)

Diet

The effect of diet on behaviour is something that very few pet owners take into consideration when they are worrying about the wayward behaviour of their dogs. It is my experience that where there is clear evidence that the dog's diet is not suitable, the behaviour will be affected to a greater or lesser degree. For example: I recently saw a young couple with a Bearded Collie called Arthur. They complained that at five years of age Arthur had started to become very aggressive towards them.

Because of an ongoing digestive problem, they had eventually settled on a diet that Arthur could manage to eat and which kept his motions fairly consistent, although occasionally he still became very loose. The owners and the referring vet were happy that at last they were getting the dog's digestive problems under control, but they had not considered the fact that his change in temperament might be related to the food.

There was clear evidence that his diet was still not suiting him. It might have been coming out at the other end in a more acceptable form (on a 'more often than not' basis), but what it was doing to him on the way through was obviously making him bad-tempered and irritable. Throughout his life he had regularly suffered from various viruses, and a wheat allergy had been diagnosed some time before. He constantly suffered from flatulence (or should I say his owners suffered from Arthur's flatulence). Although his motions were more consistent than they had been, they were still large in volume and very smelly. His activity level was extremely high and he frequently scratched his ears, nibbled his feet and legs and rubbed his eyes and nose with his feet or on the carpet. Although all of these behaviours could have some other underlying cause, added together they indicated that Arthur was not digesting his food properly and that there was a definite allergic reaction to some ingredient in his diet.

With animal nutritionist Dr Liz Parker, I had been involved for some time in a study into the effects of diet on behaviour, and Arthur seemed to be a prime candidate for participation in that survey. With the owners' agreement we tried a ten-day programme of diet therapy only — the other advice that I had given them about controlling his behaviour was not to be put into effect until after this period. A form is given to every owner who contributes to this survey, to be filled in at the end, asking them to comment on any changes and to indicate at what point they noticed a change — if at all.

When Arthur's form came back, it was accompanied by a letter — and I quote:

> There is no doubt that since we changed Arthur's diet he is like a different dog. He is just like he used to be, loving and well behaved.
>
> I was almost inclined to answer DAY 1 to the question of which day the improvement was evident, but still cannot believe it could happen so soon. [In fact they answered Day 2.]

As you suggested, we did not intend to put your advice regarding controlling Arthur's behaviour into effect until the end of the 10-day period. It now seems that there is nothing for us to do as he has already changed so much anyway.

This survey is showing what I have always suspected: that some behaviour problems can usually be improved, if not entirely cured, through carefully advised diet programmes.

Question
I have a six-year-old Hungarian Viszla bitch called Honey, who has started to act very strangely in the evening. It's as if she cannot rest and she has bouts of running around the house like she did when she was a puppy. Someone has suggested that it might be her diet, but I don't think it can be as she has always been fed on the same food, every since we have had her. What do you think it could be?

Answer
I assume that Honey has been wormed. Sometimes a heavy infestation of worms can cause a dog to charge about as if its tail was on fire, but I am sure as a dog owner of long standing you would have spotted the other signs of worms before it got to this stage. Don't necessarily rule out diet just because you have not changed the food. Sometimes the body's defence mechanisms can handle an allergen for years without any outward signs of what is happening internally. At some point, though, they are going to say 'enough is enough' and become unable to cope.

It is interesting that you say Honey behaves like this every evening — in other words, on a ritualistic basis, which would indicate a diet involvement. There are two ways of establishing this fact.

1   If she is fed once a day, change her to twice and see if you get two periods of hyperactive behaviour (same amount, split into two).
2   Change the diet. I use a high-quality, complete and balanced diet and your vet will be able to advise you on which one will best suit your dog. Alternatively, you can try a natural diet of 25 per cent white meat, 25 per cent

lightly cooked vegetables (not starchy veg) and 50 per cent boiled brown rice. If you use the latter, do not use it for too long without consulting your vet about vitamin and mineral supplementation.

Digging

In Part Two I said that wolves dig and, naturally, so do dogs. Some breeds of dogs are more prone to this behaviour than others — those in the terrier group, for instance. Northern breeds like Huskies and Malamutes are more inclined to dig cooling or sleeping hollows than other breeds, but almost any breed of dog is likely to dig for one reason or another. A dog excavates a hole with its front feet, throwing the soil under and behind, but fills it in with its nose. Some owners will have noticed that their dogs sometimes push the food bowl around the kitchen with their noses before walking away from an unfinished meal. This is a burying behaviour (part of the digging ritual) and a sure sign that they are being fed too much.

Those dog owners who are also keen gardeners (a rare combination, I admit) will know the frustration of discovering that the dog has just rearranged their carefully planted flower-beds. This is done not out of malice, but because the soil has been disturbed and the fresh scent has interested the dog — perfectly normal and extremely infuriating. The best cure is to make sure that the dog does not have access to these areas; alternatively, creating a specific area in the garden for the dedicated digger by burying toys, bones and other objects can soon centre its activities on a more acceptable patch of earth.

Question
We have a ten-year-old Border Collie bitch called Mitzy. We have had her ever since she was a puppy and she has been a dream dog until recently. The problem is that she has started to dig up the kitchen floor, initially under her usual sleeping place, which is by the door and over one of the heating pipes where she is nice and warm. Then she started on the tiles a few feet away. Now she has tried to dig holes right across the kitchen. This started around last November, and my husband has managed to catch her at it a couple of times when he has had to get up early for work, but even though he was very cross with her, she continues to do it. We don't want her to sleep in the lounge,

in case she starts on the carpet. Is there anything we can do to
stop her?

Answer
I would suggest that you bleed your central heating system.
The fact that she sleeps over one of the pipes and started the
digging activity there; the fact that you say she has dug holes
across the kitchen floor and not all over it; the fact that it started
around November, the time of year when most people set their
heating systems to come on before they get up; the fact that
your husband has caught her at it early in the morning — all
these would suggest that there is some underground activity
which Mitzy is trying to investigate. It might be air in the
system to us, but it is probably a mole to your dog. (NB. I
received a phone call: After giving this advice they had bled the
system, there was air in it, and Mitzy was no longer digging.

Dominance
Whenever anybody talks about a dominant dog, it always con-
jures up pictures of an aggressive dog, but this is not necessarily
so. Of course, a dog that has a dominant character is more
likely to become aggressive if any person, or any dog, tries to
challenge its position, but this is usually seen in dogs that have
inherited the dominant trait (through the genes of their parents). Some dogs exhibit what I call 'passive dominance'. If
challenged they do not necessarily show aggression; they
become extremely disobedient and hyperactive — they act the
fool. We really should examine what we mean by dominance
before we pursue the subject any further.

The dictionary definition says: *Dominate: Having commanding
influence over; be the most influential or conspicuous; have commanding
position.*

Some of the dogs that I see meet this definition perfectly.
They are reported to be disobedient; overwhelmingly friendly
towards visitors; eager to greet all the people that they meet
outside; always getting under people's feet inside, but have a
lovely temperament. Within the household they are the most
influential and hold the most commanding position because
everyone's attention is taken up in trying to control them. If you
told your dog to get off your bed and it growled at you, you
would recognise it as a dominant dog. With the passive dominant dog, you tell it to get off your bed and it sticks its bum up

in the air in a play posture. When you grab its collar to drag it off, it throws itself on its back and tries to wrap its legs around your arms. When it is unceremoniously dumped on the floor, it gets up and does three or four laps of the bedroom before jumping back on the bed with a playful 'woof'. It is hard not to smile and think, the dog's an idiot, but in fact it has done exactly what the aggressive dog has done — it has said NO.

Dominance is therefore more a state of mind than anything else. If the dog viewed you as more dominant than himself, whether his dominance was hereditary or because he had been granted too many privileges (see Chapter 3), then he would get off the bed when told to do so — in fact, he probably would not have got on it in the first place. Trying to dominate a dog through training might well have some success with the passive type which has inadvertently been granted this position, but with the genetically inherited aggressive type it will create a confrontation. Regardless of the type of dominance, it is always better to demote the dog in the den (at home) first. This can be done on a non-confrontational basis simply by establishing some of the rules mentioned in Chapter 3. If the dog's state of mind accepts that you hold the higher rank, training him becomes much easier. If you were really honest about it, you would agree that training dogs to sit and stay or walk to heel is just teaching them a trick. Having the right to tell your dog when to perform that trick, regardless of the distractions around him, depends upon whether he sees that you have the rank to do so.

Question
Why does my dog cock his leg so much? He is a three-year-old St Bernard and was castrated at 15 months because he had a genetic eye problem and could not be used for breeding. I am certain that he is not territory marking because he is not aggressive with other dogs, he does not mark the same places each time and he never does it when he is off the lead. In fact, the only time he does do it is after I have checked him to stop him pulling so much. I am not a large person and he is a very large dog, so even though I have him on a choke chain, he seems totally to ignore my commands and efforts to stop him pulling.

Answer

He is not ignoring your efforts to stop him pulling, that's why he is cocking his leg. Hormone status aside, leg-cocking is a dominant gesture — in this case, a sort of canine 'up yours'. Because your efforts to stop him involved strength, plus a certain amount of discomfort, and are not having the desired effect, you are proving to your dog that he is stronger than you are. Each time you attempt to control him physically, he will cock his leg almost as a gesture of defiance. My advice is to consider his behaviour around the home first, especially when it comes to who goes through doors first, eats first, or sleeps in the best places. Once you are happy that you are being granted the privileges of rank, the attitude of wanting to be out in front will be reduced. I suggest you use a Col-leash to stop him pulling because these do not require any strength (*see* Appendix). If there is no competition, he cannot win anything. If he does not win, there is no reason to give a victory squirt.

E

Epilepsy

This book is in no way intended to suggest that I have any medical knowledge, nor should any of the answers that I give in any part of the book be used as a substitute for proper veterinary care. If your dog is undergoing treatment of any kind and you would like to try some of the techniques that I describe to help with the problem, you should consult your vet first.

Epilepsy is not a behavioural problem; it is a medical problem and an hereditary condition. The reason why I have included it is because over the last two or three years I have noticed that behaviour modification programmes designed for dogs which are epileptic, whose owners have consulted me about some other problem, have reduced the number of fits from which the dog suffers. The following extract from a letter I received recently is a case in point.

> You were right: Prinz was top dog — pack leader, call it what you like — he had me well and truly under his control! I almost can't believe the magic of your training discs, they're incredible. [*See* Appendix — Sound Aversion Therapy].
>
> I'm sure you remember Prinz because of his epilepsy and his primary resistance to the training discs — he obviously didn't want to be demoted from his pack leader position. But he is. Just picking up the discs makes both Nero and Prinz like putty in my hands. Prinz immediately retires to his new position in the kitchen and Nero sits down like greased lightning.
>
> The dogs are definitely more secure and less demanding, but the real spin-off (a miracle, I reckon) is that Prinz's fits have improved dramatically. His previous fit pattern was approximately five-week gaps, but to date,

since consultation with yourself, he has had only one fit in 17 weeks.

My heartfelt thanks from me and my two German Shepherd Dogs.

The 'training discs' mentioned in this letter were only a part of the programme that I advised for Prinz and Nero, and I am not suggesting that increased control over a dog's behaviour can control epilepsy. My theory is as follows:

I cannot remember an occasion when a dog suffering from epilepsy has been brought to me with a problem that related to an over-attachment to its owners. As far as I can recall, every problem has been dominance-related, certainly since I have sat up and taken notice. If a dog has a predisposition towards epilepsy and also shoulders the responsibility of leader of the pack, that responsibility is going to put it under greater stress (*see* Stress, p. 197). If the dog is permanently stressed, the chances of an epileptic attack are increased. There is only one cure for stress and that is to take a holiday. By relieving the dog of the leader role, we can in effect give it a holiday. Since I recognised the significance of this, with dog after dog, the result has been a marked reduction in the fit pattern.

Escape behaviour

This problem can take two forms: one is anxiety-related, where the dog cannot stand the desolation of being left alone and will try to dig through doorways and windows to follow the owner (*see* Anxiety, p. 76). The other is the 'escape artist' who — regardless of what obstacles are placed in its way — will go under, over, or through them to escape from the confines of its territory and explore the big wide world beyond, whether the owner is there at the time or not. It is this second category that we are going to examine in this section.

The two elements that need to be explored are:

1   What is the external incentive that is encouraging the dog to escape?
2   What steps have been taken to secure the environment?

By discovering what it is that makes the dog so dedicated in its attempts to get out, we can either remove the incentive or satisfy it on our own territory. For example: if it is simply a lack of mental stimulation, increased off-territory controlled exercise can satisfy the urge that the dog is choosing to satisfy for itself. If the dog is an entire male and one of the local bitches has come into season, the problem will eventually go away on its own with that particular bitch, although he may go looking for others. The long-term cure for the escaping Romeo is castration (*see* Castration p. 92). Perhaps a neighbour has got into the habit of putting food out for the foxes or a stray cat, or even of giving your dog a biscuit when he calls round; a quiet word with them about your problem might help. Some dogs are keen to escape on just one day of the week, usually dustbin day — the practice of putting rubbish out in plastic sacks is a great temptation to a dog. The solution is to keep him in until the dustmen have been.

Alternatively, a sensible solution is to make the environment more secure. Building higher fences is not the answer for the dog that climbs out; turning the top inwards at a 45-degree angle is a much better solution. If the property is large and unfenced, you will have to build a dog-proof area in part of it.

Expecting a dog to learn to stay on your property when he is unsupervised is impossible if he has the incentive to go and the opportunity to get out. Making sure that the dog which is escaping because he is bored cannot get out is cruel if you are not prepared to offer him some alternative stimulation.

Question
We own ten acres of land right out in the country and we have two dogs, one a four-year-old Greyhound and the other a two-year-old-Dalmatian. It is impossible to dog-proof the whole area and, until recently, was not necessary. However, a few nights ago a fox appeared on our patio and we let the dogs out to chase it off. They disappeared after it, but about an hour later the fox was back and there was no sign of the dogs. They did not return until about five o'clock the following morning when we heard the Dalmatian barking.

That day, we heard that three sheep had been killed by dogs and although we did not say anything, we think it could have been our dogs. We have not allowed them to run free since then, but it seems an awful shame to have all this land and not let the dogs have the benefit of it. Do you think that this was a 'one-off' occasion, considering that we have not had this problem before?

Answer

It might well have been a 'one-off' occasion (the first time), but the bottom line is that if it was your dogs that killed the sheep, and it probably was, they will have had such a wonderful time hunting and killing that the chances of them doing it again are very high. Chasing the fox together aroused the instinct; if the sheep were disturbed by this and ran, your dogs would automatically transfer the chase to them. Contrary to popular opinion, it is not a question of having tasted blood, it is a question of dormant hunting instincts having been aroused. Your only solution is containment. Either a reasonable area that will be financially practical to dog-proof, or a larger area with the use of electric cattle fencing.

I would normally only consider advising shock therapy where the alternative is euthanasia. In your particular case, a repeat of this incident could well result in just that for both of your dogs. Fencing off a fairly substantial area and placing visual reminders (like white posts) every so often will mean that, once the dogs have learnt not to approach the fence, it can be removed and the white posts left. These will act as an on-going warning to the dogs. If you decide to opt for this method, make sure that you are present during the initial introduction and preferably with one dog at a time, to avoid confusion about what actually stung them. There is a similar, but more expensive, alternative to this called 'invisible fencing'. This consists of a wire that is buried just below the surface and carries a radio wave. The dog has to wear a special collar which has a receiver attached. As it approaches the area, a warning buzzer is sounded. If it continues to move forward, it receives a mild shock. (Details available from Invisible Fence (Wessex), Westwood House, Bradford Peverell, Dorchester, Dorset, DT2 9SE.)

Euthanasia

The death of a pet is always very sad, but something which we eventually gear ourselves up to accept as the years pass by. To have to make the decision to end its life prematurely, for whatever reason, is awful. However, as responsible dog owners, it becomes part of that responsibility to ensure that our dog, which has given us the loyalty and devotion that only a dog can give, never loses its dignity or suffers because we have not got the courage to make the final decision. My reason for including this section (for which there can be no question and answer) is for the reader who has had this choice to make, made it for the good of the dog and has felt guilty ever since. I myself have been faced with this choice, made it, and felt the same, so I can write this with feeling and sympathy.

A dog is the only love that money can buy — sometimes, we have to repay this love at the expense of our own emotions. People who hesitate in making what is usually an inevitable decision do so for two reasons. The first is selfish: they would not be able to stand the heartache. The second is ridiculous: humans have this belief that things will work out in the end. At the end of the day, the dog knows no difference. People do not hesitate to sign a disclaimer if their dog needs an anaesthetic for surgery, yet the procedure is exactly the same as for euthanasia, only on these occasions our conscience is clear, we are doing it for the good of the dog. Nobody who reads this book has ever had a dog put down for anything other than that reason — the good of the dog — they would not bother to read a book like this if they had.

When our dogs lose their dignity and quality of life, they rely on us to help them. We use our superior knowledge to try every avenue available to prolong and improve their lot. At the end of the day, there is only one person who can make the final choice, and the more that person grieves, the more the dog was loved when it was alive. That surely cannot be a bad epitaph?

F

Feeding

It is common practice, once a dog reaches the age of 12 months, only to feed it once a day. This probably goes back to the time when the dog was given the family's left-overs at the end of the day, and it has carried on from then. Most dogs are still growing at 12 months, in fact the majority of them do not fully develop until they are about two years old. If we are mindful that during the major growth period (up to 12 months) they need to be fed more than once a day, I cannot understand why owners blindly follow tradition and, at 12 months, cut their food down to one meal. It is usually around 12 to 14 months of age that we start to experience problems with our dogs — problems that we generally classify as normal adolescent behaviour. Any parent will tell you that when their children reach a similar stage in their development, they eat like horses. Sure, they have adolescent problems, but their behaviour is usually worse when they are hungry. I shall discuss the dog which is 12 months and over under Juvenile (p. 153).

Most breeders give the new owners a diet sheet with the puppy. This usually contains information on what type of food to feed it on and how many times it should be fed each day depending upon its age. For example:

Up to four months	4 times a day
four to six months	3 times a day
six to twelve months	twice a day
twelve months onwards	once a day

The caring pet owner will stick rigidly to this time-table, convinced that the breeder must be right because, for example, at about six months the dog starts to be a bit picky with its mid-day meal. At this age, dogs go through dormant growth periods

A few small meals are better than one big one.

and growth spurts, and at six months two meals a day might be sufficient to meet their nutritional requirements.

At seven months, however, a dog may be entering a stressful growth spurt and its body will need that extra meal. Basically, the breeder's recommendations should be taken as an average guide, not a bible. The owner should feed the growing dog in relation to its appetite and its looks (don't let it get fat, or thin).

One of the problems with some of the highly nutritional commercial pet foods that are available is that we can put too much nutrition into a growing dog too quickly. If you try and force the growth rate, especially in one of the larger, big-boned breeds, all sorts of leg joint and bone problems can result. Most of the better complete diets have different formulations for each stage of the dog's life, including the senior citizen stage, and if in doubt, your vet will advise you on which one to give to your dog.

In a similar vein, the practice of supplementing a growing dog's diet with bone meal, calcium and other vitamin and mineral supplements can actually be detrimental if you are feeding a complete and balanced diet. It is not possible to put bone where genetically there is no bone, and trying to do this by supplementing the diet will create an imbalance in the formulation — 'complete and balanced' means just that.

Going back to the practice of feeding only once a day, admittedly the majority of dogs who are fed on this regime are fit, healthy and satisfied. There is another side to the coin, though, besides the fact that at 12 months most dogs still have some growing to do. Our dogs nowadays do not have a lot to look forward to: their walks and the attention we give them. In many cases these are cut to the bare minimum because of the busy life-styles we lead. Their other daily treat is their food, so why not give them two treats a day instead of one; the same daily amount, but divided into two equal portions? There is the added benefit that, by feeding in this way, it is easier for the dog to extract the right nutrients from the food (providing they are in there in the first place) — *see* Diet, p. 106.

Giving the dog its 24-hour food supply in one bulk meal is asking its digestive system to cope with an awful lot, and the result is that a lot of goodness passes out in the faeces; stoking the boiler little and often allows the system to cope much better.

Question

My dog is a real Jekyll and Hyde character. He is a two-and-a-half-year-old German Short Haired Pointer and is extremely fit and active. He gets two one-hour runs every day, plus he has the run of our large garden, which he makes full use of. If he isn't chasing birds and squirrels, he is annoying our other dog (a five-year-old, very sedate Collie). When she makes it quite clear that she isn't interested in playing, he charges up and down the fence with the dog from next door. For the greater part of the day he is a friendly, happy-go-lucky dog, but he changes at about four o'clock when he becomes very grumpy. When you stroke him, he growls — very softly but it's there. If we scold him for it he becomes worse. If we accidentally bump into him, we get the same treatment. He is not like this at any other time of the day and someone suggested it might be his diet. I find this hard to believe because this happens before he is fed, not after. He is fed at six o'clock with the other dog, he eats very well, and if it was the food that was to blame I would have thought we would see a change of character shortly after eating. What do you think could be causing it?

Answer

I think *it is* the food that is to blame — not what you are giving him to eat — but how you are giving it to him. The type of dog that you describe (active, full of fun, always on the go) has a much higher metabolic rate than your 'laid back' Collie. This means that the energy-giving ingredients in the food are going to be burnt up much quicker than with a dog that has a ploddy nature. What is causing your dog to appear grumpy in the late afternoon is 'hunger tension'.

Accepting the fact that the dog's forefather, the wolf, survives on a 'gorge and starve', eating regime, we think that our domestic dog can easily adapt to this. Some 'died-in-the-wool' dog people still starve their dogs on one day a week. This is one of the areas where the difference between the wolf in the wild and the modern domestic dog becomes apparent. By feeding on a daily basis, we educate the system to expect a regular intake. Starving the dog on one day lowers the blood sugar level and makes the dog irritable — to say nothing of the symptoms that it may feel and is unable to tell us about. We get headaches, feel cold, get hunger pangs. Dogs that have a high metabolic rate may also suffer from these symptoms on a daily basis. Changing to a twice-daily feeding routine will ensure that your dog's tank will be full of petrol whenever he needs to use it.

Fighting

There is probably a whole army of people furtively creeping around the back streets of Britain late at night exercising their dogs. Why? Because their dogs are classified as fighters. This is one of the most distressing problems for pet owners to have to cope with, simply because, whereas they may be able to keep their dogs under leash control, the owners of dogs that 'just want to play' see nothing wrong in allowing their dogs to approach other dogs which are being led. If you are in the middle of a busy park where dogs are allowed to run free and you see an owner leading his dog — or one who calls his dog to him as soon as he spots you and your dog — it is odds on that his dog is a fighter and the behaviour of the owner should be telegraphing that fact.

In reality, the majority of dogs that are brought to me with this reported problem are not fighters in the true sense. They may not be very sociable with other dogs, they may be very dominant towards other dogs, they can sometimes be frightened of other dogs, but these attitudes do not necessarily make them fighters. Sure, they have exhibited aggressive behaviour in the past, for whatever reason, but when I ask the owners what sort of damage they have inflicted on other dogs, the answer is invariably: none. When I ask what sort of damage their dog has sustained, the answer is invariably: none. In most cases, if there are any injuries, they are usually those that the owners of the dogs involved receive during their attempts to separate the two animals.

By nature the dog is a sociable animal, but there is a variety of reasons why they become anti-social. Lack of proper early socialisation is probably the major reason why older dogs become insecure and aggressive around other dogs. If they do not learn how to behave and how to interact with other dogs during the first few formative months of their lives, they will never be confident in the presence of a strange dog. Given time, they will get used to dogs that they meet on a regular basis, but the problems arise with the chance encounters, especially with dogs of the same sex. The way that the owners handle these situations can either improve the dog's behaviour or make it worse. Quite often, the initial aggressive behaviour is designed to tell the other dog, 'I am not happy in your presence and I would prefer it if you hopped it.' The owner comes rushing in, shouting, screaming and sometimes lashing out with the lead or his feet. By his own aggressive response, he can turn an aggressive display on the part of the dog into real aggression. It only takes three or four repetitions to turn an unsociable dog, which is basically intolerant of the attentions that other dogs pay to him, into a dog-aggressive fighter. Very rarely will this type of dog approach other dogs, it prefers to avoid them. If it is impossible to do so, it will generally exhibit a very aggressive posture which is designed to tell the other dog that it has no wish to interact. Left to their own devises, the two dogs will come to an agreement with no escalation of the hostility, but we panic and spoil it all.

As a result, these dogs are then leash-walked only. The restriction of the lead makes it even more impossible for the unsociable dog to take avoiding action and therefore its only form of defence is to display aggression.

Without realising it, the owner is now embarking upon a training programme which is designed to make his dog lethal in the presence of others. A vicious circle has been created and, in most cases, a punishment-orientated routine is adopted by the owner in an attempt to stop the aggression. All that the dog learns from this is that the presence of another dog is a prelude to punishment, so it is good canine insurance to warn the other dog off. For this it is punished, which further convinces the dog that he was right in the first place.

The dog's diet can also play a key role in his behaviour around other dogs, and in most cases of dog-to-dog aggression some diet therapy is called for (*see* Diet, p. 106). Where the situation has reached the problematical level of the owner joining the ranks of the midnight dog walkers, the biggest problem to overcome is the owner's lack of confidence. Telling him that it is highly unlikely that his dog will actually fight if it is given the freedom to avoid the other dog does nothing to reassure him —

he wants proof. Changing from a short, restrictive lead and choke chain onto an extending lead with a broad leather collar, so that the dog's critical distance is extended and there is no pain-associated problem involved, usually has a visual calming effect on this type of dog. Once the owner can see by the change in the dog's behaviour that his own reaction and the way that he has handled the problem have heightened the aggression, we can usually progress to some off-leash activity.

Initially, for safety and to boost the owner's confidence, the dog is fitted with a soft nylon muzzle (Mikki Muzzle). The dog to which it is to be introduced is specially selected for temperament and confidence and the area of introduction is neutral. The owner is fully briefed to do nothing other than let dogs be dogs. Providing nobody interferes, they will either agree to play or agree to ignore each other. Rarely is there an aggressive confrontation and even then it is only very brief and always just a display. This initial introduction is very traumatic to most owners who have, by this time, convinced themselves that their dog has become a killer. The realisation that it has not is the first step to rehabilitation.

If fighting with strange dogs is distressing to the owners, fighting with other dogs in the home is intolerable. Just one or two fights usually result in both dogs being kept apart, and the pressure that this puts on the owners and the rest of the family is tremendous. Making sure that two dogs living in the same house do not meet is almost impossible. Sooner or later someone is going to leave a door open and the chances of another fight are inevitable. This enforced isolation from each other will heighten the tension between them and very serious damage can result from any future confrontation. The owners of two fighting dogs have limited options. Either re-home one of the dogs, or cure the problem. Keeping them separate is not an option if the family are to be taken into consideration.

Curing the problem can sometimes be incredibly easy. Here again, it is usually the owner's over-reaction that makes a problem worse. Two dogs have a spat, which the owner manages to stop. Whatever the argument was about has not been allowed to be resolved, so they have another spat. Again it is stopped, in the belief that they are fighting to the death, and the dogs are separated. If this enforced isolation goes on for long and they manage to meet, they probably will fight to the death. So what has started as a minor disagreement has been escalated by the owner into a major war. Providing they are initially not causing serious injury to each other, it is better to let the dogs sort out their disagreement between them.

If you have been isolating your dogs and want to get them back together again, then re-introduce them on totally neutral territory. Once they are comfortable with each other again, the garden is the next area where they should meet. Finally the house, but make sure that there is a door open to give one of the dogs an escape route should it be needed. Dogs that have lived together in the past, and who start to argue, usually have a reason which can be resolved between them, providing we allow them to do so.

Question

I have two Border Terrier dogs, one of 18 months and the other 21 months. They are half-brothers from different bitches but both have the same father. They have always got on well together until recently when they have started to fight over the least little thing. Toys, foods, beds — they even started a fight when I stroked the older one and the young one started to push in. I knew it was not a good idea to get two brothers, but I wanted two of the same breed as near in age as I could get them, so that they could grow up together and be company for each other.

It has been suggested that if I have them castrated it will stop them fighting. Can you offer me any advice, please?

Answer

It sounds to me like a dominance problem, with each dog thinking that it is higher ranking than the other. This usually resolves itself and an established dominance/submissive order is achieved. However, if the problem is ongoing and you are not interfering and stopping them from reaching an agreement, then they are both genetically of equal rank — that is, both naturally dominant dogs. The problems that you tried to avoid by not taking two brothers or sisters from the same litter you have come up against with two dogs from different litters. If this is the case, then having both of them castrated is not going to do any good at all. Hormonally, they are both equal; castrate both of them and they will still be equal. However, if you can decide which of the two might just have the rank advantage, no matter how slight, and have the other one castrated, the chances are that you will create a clear-cut rank structure. Once this has been done, you can help further by favouring the entire male. Feed him first, greet him first, give him all privileges first, without allowing him to think he is higher than you. Although some people do not agree, I have found that in a lot of similar cases where the problem involves two bitches, spaying one of them can help — especially in a mother-daughter relationship. (*see* Spaying, p. 194).

Games

All dogs learn through play. I am not talking about the formal learning process of Heel, Stay, Sit and Come, although if we can make these exercises into a fun-type game the dog will learn to perform them much quicker. I am talking about the learning process of how to be a dog.

If you think about the type of games that your dog loves to play more than any other, you will be able to categorise them into the following groups:

Strength games: Tug-of-war, rough-and-tumble, etc.
Possession games: Steal the sock, hide the toy, bury the bone, etc.
Chase games: Steal the shoe and invite you to get it back; chase the ball or stick and invite you to *try* and get it back.
Killing games: Shake the rag, slipper, stick, etc.

All these games are designed to establish dominance and to teach hunting and killing skills. They are games that all dogs play and they are instinctive. Humans play games to amuse themselves in their spare time, dogs play to learn. It is important, therefore, that we understand the significance of these games if we are going to play them with our dogs on a regular basis.

The names of the games give us a clue to what they are all about. There are tug toys available in pet shops that give the human one end to hold and the dog the other. What we don't realise is that the dog will never give in when we play this game with him. Either we stop playing it because it is getting out of hand and the dog is becoming too excited and aggressive, or the phone has rung, or someone has knocked at the door. Alternatively, we admire the dog's tenacity and dedication, so we reward him by letting him pull it out of our hands. What we have done is accept the challenge to test strength for strength, and lost. In fact we have encouraged the competition, by buying a specially designed toy in the first place.

Having won the game, the dog will invariably take the toy to his bed, or to a favourite corner of the room. This is to signify that he is now in possession of that article — he has won it in fair combat and it is now his trophy, the victor's reward. Just like human rewards, it is a visual sign of superiority. If we don't invite dogs to play this game, they learn how to invite us. For example, you get one sock on your foot and then look around for the other. Where is it? In the dog's mouth. We go to get it back and the dog runs off. We chase him and eventually we get our sock back. We have won this game, but we are now convinced that the dog likes socks, so we give him some old socks to play with. We don't really want these back, so in every subsequent game of 'get the sock' the dog will win.

A variation on this game of possession involves the 'trophying' of more valuable items. If the dog picks up an old piece of wood, or waste paper, we might not take any notice. If, however, it picks up one of our best shoes, we do take notice and the chase game commences. Over a period of time, on a trial and error basis, the dog will learn just which articles result in your attention and which don't. Basically, the articles which are important are the ones that most heavily contain your scent. Throwing the ball, which has been in your pocket, becomes an article to be competed for and won by the dog. We therefore encourage: chase me games, chase after the prey games and, subsequently, more possession games.

Watching the dog growl and shake an article is great fun. Even the most novice of pet owners immediately recognises this as an instinctive killing behaviour. Again, because we find it cute — especially in the young dog — we encourage it. We give it a rag with knots in the end, watch the dog kill it and then challenge it by trying to get it off him as an invitation to play. There is no way that, having just pounced upon and killed his victim, he is going to give it up. We don't really want it, we are just teasing, but the dog does not know this. Once again he wins. He has chased, he has pounced, he has killed, he has been challenged, and he has won. Is this what we should really be teaching our dogs?

With a lot of dogs, it doesn't really matter. They will play these games simply because they are dogs, but they do not take advantage of the extra rank that they instinctively earn by winning them. However, if you are having problems with your dog, then you must think seriously about whether these games are an important part of the daily routine, which one of you initiates the game and, most importantly, who generally wins.

Question

We have a ten-month-old Lakeland Terrier bitch which is still very submissive towards all the family. If someone drops something or raises their voice, she runs and hides, and when we come in to the room she comes towards us in a very cringy manner and still urinates like a puppy does; even if we try to play with her, she just rolls over on her back. I don't think she is a nervous dog, because she does not act like that with strangers — just us. It is awfully embarrassing when we have friends round, it looks as though we have beaten her, which of course we have not. We knew that she was the most submissive dog in the litter, but we thought that she would have grown out of it by now. Is there anything that you can suggest to make her a bit bolder?

Answer

Because she was the most submissive one of the litter, she would have lost all the competitive games that puppies play with each other: tug-of-war, possession games, rough-and-tumble games and who can push themselves into the best sleeping and eating positions. Your bitch would have ended up as a non-competitor in the games and would have accepted the fact that she must suckle from the less lucrative teat of the mother and end up sleeping on the fringes of the pack. Normally, when they are integrated into a different environment, their confidence begins to grow because they start to win some of these games with us and we allow them certain privileges which promote their rank and build their self-esteem. Normally, I advise my clients not to grant their dogs these privileges. If they are going to play competitive games, to make sure that they — not the dog — win them all. In your case, the opposite is what I advise. The reason she will not play with you is that she is convinced she will lose.

Your friends are not part of her pack, so she can compete with them in the normal way because they are not her peers. You and your family have become an extension of her first pecking-order experience, which can sometimes happen, especially if you went to look at her fairly often, prior to her being old enough to leave her natural mother. You need to boost her confidence. Start with a ten-second game which involves a tug toy or rag. Don't expect her to pull it: she won't because she will be convinced that she can't win. If she puts her teeth on it at all, let go and walk away. After a few repetitions, her efforts will become more committed as her confidence grows. For a short period of time, you and the rest of the family must lose all competitive games. The more she wins, the less submissive she will be towards you — but be careful! You need only strike a happy medium, not encourage a takeover bid. (*See also*, Submissiveness, p.199).

Grooming
Whether your dog is short-coated or long-haired, daily grooming is essential for the following reasons:

1 It stimulates the skin to produce vital protective oils.
2 It gives early warning of any impending skin problems or injury.
3 It obviously makes long-coated dogs feel better and has the same effect on short-coated dogs as it does on us when we have a good scratch in the morning — it's a good feeling.
4 It establishes us as the dominant animal in the relationship.

Points 1 to 3 are basically self-explanatory, except for the fact that because of our modern, centrally heated environments, there is no longer the need for a lot of dogs to have the 'vital protective oils'. These oils will build up naturally, causing greasy marks on our wallpaper and obnoxious smells in very warm rooms. As a result, we buy one of the commercially available shampoos to clean the dog.

But are we being fair on the dog? Come the winter months, we still keep them in a warm environment, we wash off the protective oils and then we take them out into freezing temperatures for exercise.

We will wrap up warmly for the transition from one temperature to another, but only the toy breeds (usually) are granted the same consideration.

Providing the dog's diet is correct (a lot of skin trouble and 'dog aroma' is diet-related); providing the dog is not housed constantly in an 80-degree environment; providing its coat and skin are stimulated regularly through grooming — there should be no need for regular bathing. If your wallpaper and door frames are getting soiled by dog grease, however, bathing does become necessary, but it should be kept to a minimum, especially in the winter months.

Point 4 is one of the most important side-effects of regular daily grooming. In a wolf pack, grooming is an important aspect of social interaction, although the thick, dense coat of the wolf is very different from many of the coats that the modern domestic dog has evolved. The wolf's coat is unlikely to mat and two rapid moults a year take care of any tangles that do develop. The thinner, longer hair of the dog does have a tendency to mat and therefore needs the care that only we are capable of giving. As far as we and the dog are concerned, the major benefits obtained by regular grooming are that it establishes a regular social interaction and confirms the pack bond between us, and, by paying particular attention to grooming around the socially significant areas like the ears, top of neck and withers, tail and feet, we are establishing ourselves as the more dominant animal.

Question

I have a long-haired Dachsund which hates being groomed, in fact he can become quite aggressive. I have to take him to a professional grooming parlour and they say that they never have any trouble with him, although I think they use a muzzle. I should be able to groom him myself, but every time I try it develops into an argument between us. How can I teach him to stand still and not bite?

Answer

The professionals probably do use a muzzle, and if your dog is likely to bite it is a very sensible precaution to take. It may be that when he was young you inadvertently hurt him by trying to sort out one of his tangles. If he snapped at you and you stopped grooming, he would have learnt that he can stop you quite easily. As the time wore on, as you have stated, this has developed into an ongoing argument between you. Now, when you pick up a grooming brush or comb, it is a prelude to an unpleasant situation. No doubt he tried to pull the same stunt

Have him groomed professionally.

with the professional groomer, but, being muzzled, could do no harm and was probably firmly told to 'quit it' whilst the grooming continued.

It would be no good you trying that approach on its own; the problem will have become too deep-rooted. What you need to do is to desensitise your dog to accept being groomed as a prelude to a pleasant and not an unpleasant situation. Start by having him groomed professionally, so that there are no tangles that have to be sorted out, and ask your grooming parlour to supply you with a muzzle for your own protection. Tether him by his collar and leash to something secure to stop him running off. Place your hand under his belly, below the rib cage, so that if he struggles you can gently lift his hindquarters off the ground. Gently brush his back about a dozen times (because he will just have been groomed properly, your intention is simply to get him to accept you brushing him). Ignore all of his attempts to object, don't even tell him off, and praise all passive behaviour — you do not want to perpetuate the argument (which is why you should not scold him). Release him and reward him, either with a particularly juicy tit-bit or part of his daily food ration.

Continue this procedure regularly, until he accepts that being groomed is actually a good thing — he gets paid nice attention when he stands still and gets rewarded at the end. Remember that the initial object is not to groom him, it is to get him to accept the procedure of grooming.

Guarding

To guard is a natural instinct in most breeds of dog, although some have a more enhanced instinct and are better equipped physically to be more successful at it. It is their usefulness at guarding that probably started the man/dog relationship in the first place. When stone age people huddled round the light of their fires, the wild packs that hung around the fringes, feeding off the discarded food of the humans, would have given warning of approaching danger. People probably encouraged these packs to follow them from hunting ground to hunting ground by leaving a trail of food for them. Perhaps one of the children found a stray cub or an abandoned litter, and brought them into the camp and raised them — the first of many domesticated guards.

Their usefulness as an aid to hunting would have been discovered later, but it was their guarding abilities initially that proved their worth. It is no different today, regardless of the size of the dog; their ability to give early warning is still one of the major reasons why our relationship continues. During my service as a professional dog handler, a burglar once told me that it was not the size of the dog that worried him, it was the fact that it might bark and wake up the household.

Sometimes, this natural instinct becomes a problem, especially when the dog starts to guard things from the family with whom it lives, or guards the family from people to whom we want to speak, or visitors whom we have invited. In almost every case of this kind, the dog has achieved pack leader status and sees it as his or her role to be the protector and decision-maker, instead of one of the lower ranks whose job it is to be the look-out and give warning. If your dog falls into this category, Chapter 3 should be of some use to you.

Accelerated guarding instincts that have reached a problematical level can arise for a variety of reasons. Breed-specific behaviour naturally has to be allowed for — that is, guarding breeds guard — nevertheless, it should still be under the owner's control.

Accepting the fact that we can inadvertently promote our dogs to a rank higher than we had intended, other contributory factors need to be considered — hereditary behaviour, for example. If both the mother and the father had a reputation for being aggressive guarding types, then the chances are that there is not a lot you can do about the behaviour of the offspring. The dog's diet needs to be looked at, too; the case of Arthur, mentioned in the diet section (p.106), is a classic example of how the behaviour of the dog can be affected. Learned behaviour is also a very important contributory factor. Most dogs develop this natural guarding instinct as they reach maturity, without any help from us. Because one of the reasons for obtaining the dog might well have been as a protector of property, perhaps the owners encouraged the dog to show aggression at an early age, only to find that it got out of hand when the natural instinct arose. In these cases, some of the aversive techniques mentioned in the Appendix can prove useful. Lack of early experience will inevitably result in a lack of confidence, therefore the guarding behaviour is not the dog protecting us, it is the dog protecting itself.

Whatever the extenuating circumstances, it should be remembered that the instinct to guard is natural. If the dog is one of the large guarding breeds, whose behaviour was encouraged as a puppy, has attained a high rank within its domestic environment and whose diet is also unsuitable, the owner has a big, but not insurmountable problem. To bring the behaviour under control, all these factors need to be considered before a rehabilitation programme can be devised.

Question

Why does my dog (Becky) take all the toys to her bed and guard them — never plays with them — while the other dog (Sally) quietly chooses one toy and takes it to her bed to play with and chew at? Becky is sometimes so bad that she goes up to Sally and barks at her because she wants the particular toy that Sally has.

Also, when Sally leaves her toy for any reason, Becky will race up to it, pick it up and carry it back to her bed to 'guard' with the others. Becky and Sally are litter sisters and have always been treated the same, so why are they so different?

Answer

It is not unusual for two dogs from the same litter to be as different as chalk is from cheese. In fact, it is as well that they are. If they were both alike, the chances are that they would be constantly fighting for the position of top dog. That is exactly the statement that Becky is making by trophying all the toys. She is making it clear to Sally that she is the higher-ranking dog and is therefore entitled to all possessions. Sally obviously recognises this fact, otherwise you would be asking how to stop your dogs fighting whenever there was a toy around. If you were to remove all the toys, Becky would find some other way of exhibiting her higher rank over Sally and this might take a form that would be far less acceptable to you.

Providing Becky is only guarding toys from Sally and not from you, I would be inclined to sit back and just observe how easily dogs can establish rank structures without having to resort to violence. Whilst you are watching perfectly normal canine behaviour in action, consider how nice it would be if humans were able to do the same.

H

Heelwork
See Pulling, p.167.

Herding

Watching a herding dog at work is a wonderful sight, but you don't have to go to a farm or tune in to 'One Man and his Dog' on television to see these dogs at their work. Just pay a visit to your local park or, in many cases, observe your own dog's behaviour. To herd is another natural instinct in all dogs, but some have obviously been specifically bred from over the years because of their highly developed herding instinct. From these we get the dogs that we recognise as being one of the herding breeds. One of the questions that I ask my clients is, 'When you let your dog off its lead in the park, does it run away from you?' Very rarely do I get a 'yes' answer. More often than not I am told that it does, but not very far, that it keeps running back to check that they are following and then runs off again. When I ask them to describe exactly what it does, they generally agree that the dog runs off, comes back and goes behind them on one side, before running off again on the other side. When further questioned they agree that the dog keeps this up throughout the walk. It is not checking that the owners are following, it is herding them along.

This herding behaviour during a walk is a classic sign of a dominant dog — unless of course it is one of the herding breeds and then it borders on breed-specific behaviour. These same dogs will be accused of following the owners around the house, but again, after asking them to examine exactly what the dog does, they usually agree that it is generally in front of them most of the time. Visitors to the house normally receive the same treatment, which most owners put down to over-friendliness.

In fact the dog is basically restricting the freedom of movement of these visitors, which is the object of herding.

Although behaviour problems cannot be categorised as such, once the owners and dogs have settled in my office, the dogs fall into three basic groups:

> Dogs that exhibit anxiety-related problems, like house-soiling, destructiveness, howling and barking, will generally stay very close to the family.

> Dogs that exhibit dominance problems of a protective nature will generally lie directly between myself and the family, but keep their eye on me. Alternatively, they will take up position near the door.

> Dogs that herd their owners and exhibit dominance problems of a passive nature still take up position between me and the family, but keep their eye on the family. These dogs usually get 10 out of 10 for the pen (penning the sheep in a sheep dog trial).

These behaviours are predictable, depending upon the reported problem. I have observed them in dog after dog over a number of years and in fact the furniture in my office is set out in such a way that it allows the dog to behave in one or other of these ways if it wants to do so. Initially, I thought it was coincidence, now I know it is not, and their behaviour helps me to confirm my diagnoses of the root cause of the problem that my questions and their answers have led me to suspect.

Herding, therefore, is not restricted to collies and the like, although it is more easily recognised and accepted as normal in these breeds. All breeds of dog will herd to some degree, especially if they have been put into a leader position by the family. Whether it is natural within the breed or a side-effect of rank, the information contained in Chapter 3 will show you how to reduce the behaviour if it has become a problem.

Question

I feel so sorry for my four-year-old Border Collie called Blue: he spends all of his time herding either shadows on the wall or floor, goldfish in the pond, or our two cats. If we stop him doing one thing, he goes straight on to the other. It doesn't matter how much exercise we give him, as soon as he comes home he goes back to work. We would hate to lose him, but we feel that it is unfair to keep him as he should be working sheep on a farm.

Answer
First of all, you would be lucky to find a farmer who would take on a four-year-old dog for sheepdog work; they generally like to have them as puppies and run them on with an older dog. But why worry? Blue sounds as if he has enough work to do as it is. Providing he is getting enough off-territory exercise, what you are seeing is the collie's highly developed working instinct, and he obviously thinks he is doing a good job. It would be unfair to stop him because he would become frustrated and this would result in other problems arising. Providing you, the cats, the goldfish and the shadows don't mind, you can rest assured that sheep would be no different to Blue — they are just something to be herded. It sounds to me as though your dog is luckier than most domestic dogs; at least he has an outlet for his instincts and I am sure he is perfectly happy in his job.

Hereditary behaviour
All too often I am told that nothing can be done about a dog's behaviour because either the sire or the dam was the same — in other words the problem has been genetically acquired and you cannot change an animal's genes. This, of course, is perfectly true, but genetically acquired behaviour patterns are quite often different from hereditary behaviour.

Puppies learn at an incredible rate during the first few weeks of life, in fact by about seven to eight weeks they are transmitting adult brain waves. A lot of their behaviour is copied — monkey see, monkey do. If a bitch is aggressive to strangers, then it is likely that the puppies will copy her behaviour. If that bitch had become aggressive because she was never socialised properly, or her diet was all wrong, for instance, then the puppies' behaviour has not been genetically acquired, it has been learned. Behaviour inherited through the genetic make-up of the parents is unalterable; inheriting the behaviour through a learned process can be altered. In both cases, the behaviour has been passed from one generation to another and so, strictly speaking, it is hereditary. But as you can see, it does not necessarily mean that it cannot be changed.

Whenever I am told by the owners that 'the mother was the same', in the absence of the mother I always assume that the mother's problem could have been cured, and that therefore my patients' can, too. If I do not take this approach, I would be admitting defeat before we started and it is very pleasing when a complete cure is effected. Where we only manage to control the problem, then it probably was genetic.

The number of problem dogs that have been initially diagnosed as being 'like father, like son' and who have been completely rehabilitated is quite high, which goes to show that we are often too quick to blame breeding for our inability to exercise proper control or to consider other extenuating circumstances.

Question

I have a two-year-old Golden Cocker Spaniel dog who is very possessive, especially over his food. He is almost as bad with toys, in fact anything that he can get hold of. His aggression is quite frightening although he has never actually bitten. I have been told that this is an hereditary condition called 'Cocker Rage Syndrome' and that it is more often seen in the golden colour. We don't really want to have him put to sleep, but if we cannot stop him, we will have to do so before he does bite somebody. Can you advise me, please?

Answer

Rage Syndrome, whether exhibited by the Cocker Spaniel or any other breed, is an 'in phrase'. Rightly or wrongly, I define rage as being sudden and violent aggression for no apparent reason. You have said that there is a reason for your dog's behaviour — possession. You have also stated that he has never bitten and so, ferocious as it might seem, it is controlled. Controlled aggression for a specific reason would not be classified as rage in my opinion.

It is true that Cocker Spaniels have become renowned for this kind of behaviour, but it is not confined to the Golden. It does, however, seem to be more prevalent in the whole colours (Goldens, Blacks, Liver, Red) but not so much in the mixed colours (Black and Tan, Black and White, Blue Roan).

There is a theory that the gene that dictates colour might also be responsible for fiery temper, and the popular belief regarding ginger-headed people or chestnut mares, and my own experience of tortoiseshell cats, would seem to bear this out. Having a fiery temper, though, is quite different from 'Rage

Syndrome'. I know that the Cocker Spaniel Club are doing a lot of investigation into the problems within the breed, and if it is a genetically acquired trait I am sure that they will eventually isolate and eradicate it.

Providing there are no young children in the house, who might inadvertently trigger off this possessive aggression and who are naturally more at risk, it is worth trying the following procedures:

1 Change the diet to a complete food which can be fed dry and on a free choice basis — that is, it is left down all the time and topped up regularly. Because it is a dry diet, it is far more bland than say, tinned food, and this will reduce the guarding instinct. It also means that every approach towards the bowl is to give, and not what the dog thinks, to take.

2 Remove all of the dog's toys, except one. This should be available only under your strict control and, at the end of the game, you will repossess that toy. It will help to have a trailing light line on the dog during these games, so that if he does 'trophy' the toy, you can gently remove him from it, rather than the other way round. If you have to do this, the toy is then put away immediately and the game stops. If he manages to get hold of anything else and you do not have him under the control of the line, walk out of the room as if you haven't noticed — do not accept his challenge.

3 A rearrangement of the pecking order would seem to be called for. Make sure that you are granted all the privileges of rank. *See* Chapter 3.

4 Introduce your dog to one of the sound aversion techniques mentioned in the Appendix, so that any displays of aggression over valuable articles can be interrupted without having a confrontation.

5 If there are children involved, I would strongly advise you to ask your vet to refer you to a member of the Association of Pet Behaviour Counsellors, who will assess your dog and recommend a treatment programme for your particular needs. This will be more specific than can be advised here.

House-training

One of the first lessons that puppy owners embark upon is trying to teach their new pup how to be clean in the house. This is done at a time when you are also trying to form some sort of bond with the pup, and therefore it is important that the method employed does not in any way affect your future relationship. The 'old wives' tale' of rubbing the pup's nose in the mess that he has made is cruel! It does not work! And it definitely affects the future relationship! All the puppy is ever going to learn from this is that the presence of a mess on the floor and a human at the door is bad news. Having learnt this, he shows submission when you enter the room. This submissive body language is taken as a look of guilt because 'he knows he has done wrong'. Because we believe puppies know right from wrong we assume that by punishing them they will learn in the future. They do not 'know they have done wrong'. All the time the mess is on the floor, it is no problem to the puppy; all he does is to walk round it or step over it. The mess only becomes a problem when a human arrives, sometimes hours after it had been deposited there. Seeing the mess, the human becomes cross, the puppy shows submission and the whole vicious circle is created. If this procedure continues for long, anxiety builds up in the dog about what will happen when the owner comes home. One of the side-effects of anxiety is a loss of sphincter and bowel control and as a result the problem becomes worse.

Some people who have used the 'rub their noses in it' method in the past will swear that it worked because their dogs became house-trained. They are not taking into account that the dog would have learnt anyway — much like the example quoted under fouling in Chapter 5.

If the majority of dogs, left to their own devices, eventually become house-trained, then all that we need to do is to speed the process along. To do this, we should use a system known as 'target training'.

Select an area in the garden where you want your dog to go — somewhere out of the way and on a terrain that is easily cleanable. At the times when your dog or puppy is most likely to want to go, take him to this area and wait. At first you might have to wait some time, especially if, prior to commencing this type of training, you have tried a punishment-orientated method to teach right from wrong. Your dog or puppy might have learnt that to deposit a mess when you are watching is bad news. However, if you take him to the target area first thing in the morning, shortly after feeding, or as soon as he wakes up from a nap during the day, then the chances are he is going to have to relieve himself. As soon as he does, he should be rewarded with praise and a nice juicy tit-bit — not when he gets back to the house, actually on the target area. If you ignore the fact that he has gone anywhere else, he will very quickly learn that going in one area brings reward, going anywhere else does not. Of course, if you catch him in the act of going in the wrong place, it is all right to scoop him up with a harsh BAAAD DOG, and take him to the chosen area. There is no need for physical punishment — verbal disapproval is good enough. If you are more than two seconds after the act, then neither praise nor punishment will have the desired effect.

Question
Why does my dog continue to mess in the house? He is a four-year-old Dobermann dog which we obtained in South Africa when he was a puppy. He was kept in a kennel over there and obviously spent six months in quarantine kennels when we moved to England, so I understand that he is used to just going when he wants. The problem is that we now live in a flat and, try as we might, we just cannot stop him going wherever he chooses indoors. We scold him for it, but he just seems to be getting more and more confused. Can you suggest a method which will help him to learn that outside is where he should be going?

Answer
There will be two places indoors where he definitely will not go — in his bed and where he eats. You are right that the cause of the problem is the unsupervised confinement of a kennel, but if you look at what he actually learnt himself during these years, it will give you a clue to how to start to re-train him. He would have left his sleeping or eating area and urinated and defected as far away from them as his kennel run allowed him. What you must create is two distinct areas:

1 A sleeping/eating area.
2 An exercise area.

The way to do this is to introduce him to an indoor kennel

(see Appendix, Indoor Kennels). Having spent so long in a kennelled environment, he will very quickly adjust to this regime. At regular intervals he should be taken from his kennel and given immediate supervised access to an outside toilet area. The moment he performs, he should be rewarded with verbal praise and a tit-bit. He can then be taken home and allowed his usual freedom, provided there is someone there to supervise. Whenever there is not, he should be left in his indoor kennel. In effect, you are taking him right back to the nest and re-educating him as if he were a puppy; the whole procedure should not take more than a week or so and the result will be well worth the time invested.

Hyperactivity

This is a very real condition in some dogs, just as it is in some people, especially children. However, in my opinion, true canine hyperactivity is when a dog is unable to stay quiet or to concentrate despite the controls placed upon it. Although many of my clients tell me that their dog is hyperactive, it usually proves to be the case that when proper control is exercised, these dogs become calm and relaxed. In these cases, the hyperactive behaviour was merely a symptom of some other cause — failure to control — and I suspect that this is also the case with a lot of children.

On the other hand, there is plenty of medical evidence to show that certain food additives can produce hyperactive behaviour in some children, and they are impossible to control until this influence is removed. Although, at the time of writing, there is no scientific evidence to support the claim, I personally believe that the same is true of some dogs.

I am involved in some research work into the effects of diet on behaviour (*see* Diet, p.106) and without question, some dogs are greatly affected in terms of their activity level by the food that they are given to eat. No amount of training or behaviour modification programmes will be of any use in these cases until the real cause of the problem is removed. Whether it is the balance of the diet or a certain ingredient in it, we are not yet able to say until all the data has been collected and analysed. Until then, when dealing with cases of hyperactivity, diet cannot be ruled out as a contributory factor.

Environmental influence is also a major factor to be taken into account (*see* Children, p.100) and, without doubt, the owner should be shown how to exercise greater control (*see* Appendix, Sound Aversion Therapy). Whatever the cause, a dog that acts in a hyperactive manner is going to exhibit behaviour problems that are far more difficult to correct than a dog that is basically calm. It is important, therefore, that before any attempt is made to rehabilitate the dog, the problem of its activity level should be addressed first.

Question

My dog goes absolutely manic when I come home from work. He throws himself at me, charges round and round the hallway, invariably knocking something over, and all the time he is barking in a stupid high-pitched tone. I have tried shouting at him, kneeing him in the chest when he jumps up, but it only seems to make him worse. How can I teach him to greet me calmly when I can't seem to break through his overexcitable attitude?

Answer

What usually causes this behaviour is warm, enthusiastic greetings from the owner when the dog was young. It is very hard to ignore a young puppy that jumps up at us when we come in, but in fact we should, because we are only condoning behaviour that will become unacceptable when he is older, as you have found to your cost. Ideally, greetings should be calm and preferably should not take place in doorways. The owners should come home and, for a minute or so, ignore the dog's demands for affection. Take your coat off and put your bags away before calling him over to you and giving him some calm, gentle attention (preferably in an inner room). In your case, the behaviour has become learned and this new regime will take longer to establish. The Sound Aversion Therapy techniques mentioned in the Appendix will help to stop the jumping, and if you ignore the charging round and round until you are ready to give the dog your attention, it will soon extinguish — shouting at him to calm down is only increasing the excitement of the greeting routine. If you adopt a calm, offhand attitude, the dog will eventually follow suit. Getting him to sit for a food reward in another room prior to stroking him and asking him what kind of a day he has had will quickly result in him going to that room and waiting, rather than running in circles round the hall. The key to successful and acceptable greeting procedures is calmness on your part.

I

Inducement

For many years there has been this old-fashioned idea in dog training circles that to use food is to resort to bribery. However, exponents of this theory will quite happily resort to toys and verbal, as well as physical, praise. What's the difference? They are all forms of inducement — an incentive to perform. I often ask the question, would you go to work week in and week out if you did not receive any payment? Of course the answer is no, so could this be classed as bribery or is it an inducement to work?

If we consider a situation where your dog is fast asleep in front of a roaring log fire and you pick up a pair of nail-clippers and call him over to you, the chances are that he will pretend he has not heard you. If you insist, he will probably come slowly with his ears flat to his head — especially, if you have made nail-clipping a traumatic experience in the past. If, however, you picked up his lead and called him, he would be there like a bullet. The difference of course is in the expected reward — the lead being more of an inducement to come than the nail-clippers. It becomes obvious, therefore, that the inducement should be sufficient to achieve the result. Anyone who cannot get a dog to work happily for praise or toys and who refuses to resort to food, because that would be bribery, is being slightly stupid. If food motivates the dog, then use it.

The main difference between an inducement and a reward is that the former is expected — a carrot, a lure — whereas the latter is not. (Reward will be discussed later under Reinforcement, p.179.) An inducement would normally be used at the start of teaching any new exercise, for example teaching a puppy the recall. By showing the puppy the food, a toy or whatever, and then calling it to you, you are giving that puppy a visual reason to come to you; eventually it will link the word of command with the action and then the inducement can be tailed off.

In Compulsion (p.103), the answer given on how to retrain the dog to go down on command is a classic example of the use of an inducement.

Inherent
See Hereditary behaviour, p.137.

Insensitive
See Sensitivity, p.190.

Instinctive
To a certain extent, Chapter 5 shows us that most of what the modern domestic dog does is purely instinctive and inherited from its wolf forefather. Therefore, before we start to consider what we are going to do about curing a particular problem, we should first ask ourselves the question, 'Why is my dog doing this?' In most cases, you will find the answer is — because it is perfectly normal, albeit unacceptable behaviour. Having established this fact, we can now ask the question, 'How can I channel my dog's instinctive behaviour into another direction?' Chase (p.95) shows two examples of this: 'First, how to transfer the fun of chasing from joggers to a ball; second, how to transfer predatorial chasing (which is usually food-related) to returning to the owner for food. With other problems, similar procedures should be followed and, provided you ask yourself the two key questions, 'What is the instinct that has become a problem?' and, 'How can I channel that instinct in a more acceptable direction?' the answer to the problem usually becomes clear.

It should be remembered, though, that all our dogs have the same instincts lying dormant within their nature; they only reach a problematical level when the instinct is encouraged and rewarded.

It is rare for any of us to do this on a conscious basis; we usually arouse the instinct without realising that we have done so. With chase problems, for instance, there are invariably children in the family and the games that they play with the puppy are normally to blame for the chase instinct becoming accelerated. Seldom do I see a case of a chase-related problem coming from a home where there are no children. If we can bear in mind when we acquire a new puppy that everything it does has a purpose and is part of a learning process, we can channel its games to suit ourselves and avoid arousing unacceptable instinctive behaviour. As the title of my last book suggests, we should *Think Dog!* right from the start.

Question

Why does my dog insist on greeting everyone by sticking his nose up between their legs? It is a habit that has become most embarrassing, not only to me, his owner, but obviously to the people that he does it to. Sometimes he can be most insistent and will not take no for an answer.

Answer

If you watch two dogs meeting and greeting in the park, you will see that anal/genital investigation is part of the normal meeting ritual in dogs. What he is doing, therefore, is perfectly normal but, I would agree, very embarrassing for all concerned. Dogs that exhibit this kind of behaviour to a problematical level are usually dogs that are of the right height to do so easily and have spent the first twelve to fourteen weeks of their lives within a kennel environment — in other words they are very doggy dogs which have grown to the right size to enable them to carry on greeting people as though they were other dogs. If, however, he has as you say become most insistent, there may be a hormonal/sexual element involved, and perhaps a quick chat with your vet about the possibility of trying some short-term anti-male hormone treatment might prove useful. Failing that, arming your visitors with a spray taste deterrent (*see* Appendix, Other Aversion Methods) is a quick and effective solution, providing he is rewarded by them for an alternative greeting behaviour like sitting down. The object is to make one form of greeting unpleasant, not for him to be wary of greeting your visitors at all.

Instructors

I have been accused on many occasions of making derogatory remarks about dog-training classes and their instructors. Let me set the record straight here and now. For sure, I shall criticise bad instructors at every opportunity, but at the same time I always make it clear that there are very many good instructors around and that these are on the increase. The reason why I pounce on every opportunity to advertise my feelings about some dog clubs is that the average pet owner believes that if someone advertises himself as a dog-training instructor, he must in some way be qualified to do so. This is not always the case and almost daily I hear horrific stories from my clients about the advice they have been given at the dog club in order to cure a problem. Recently, I heard of a case in which the RSPCA successfully closed a dog club and prosecuted the instructor for demonstrating and recommending continuing cruel treatment of a dog by its owners to cure a dog-aggression problem. They were advised to string it up in the air by its choke chain until it almost passed out, whenever it growled at another dog. This was done by the instructor in the club, but when the owner did it in the local park he was reported for cruelty by a couple who witnessed the incident. When the RSPCA examined the dog, they found red weals around its neck. The owner's defence was that he had attended the club to have his problem cured. He did not like doing what he had been told, but he had sought and paid for professional advice and was following that advice. Quite possibly, many of you would say that if he did not like it he should not have done it, but I can understand the position he was in. Many of my clients are guilty of cruelty in the name of training, not because they are cruel people, but because they have been told that they must carry out this or that form of punishment if they want to cure the problem — the inference being that if they do not do it they will have to live with the problem.

Although I am now working on a full-time basis with behaviour problems, my background experience has been gained through training dogs. As a trainer, I rejected many of the traditional 'pull 'em and push 'em' techniques and instead studied and applied more scientifically proven methods of positive reinforcement, but as a trainer my ability to spread the word that there are alternative, kinder and more successful methods available was restricted to my pupils. The great British dog-owning public was still being subjected to the kind of training that was being made available through advertisements in their local libraries, pet shops and vets. I am now fortunately in a position where I can spread the word to the pet owners that they should not necessarily accept the advice given to them if they feel that it would be detrimental to the dog. This advice would be useless if there were not a growing army of enlightened trainers around who are able to offer alternative methods to the worried pet owner.

My message therefore is clear. Dog training is at last catching up with the advances being made in other areas such as education, medicine and child care. There are still large numbers of clubs which have instructors who refuse to change with the times, and take the view that the only cure for a problem is punishment. I advertise this fact at every opportunity and encourage the owners to shop around until they find a club which uses modern techniques for training dogs. In short, I am not against dog clubs — just some of them!

Intelligence

We very often overestimate the intelligence of our dogs and, as a result, become impatient with them about their apparent refusal to learn. House-training is a classic example of this (*see* House-training, p.140) and the well-used phrase '*He knows he's done wrong*' bears out our misconception about the limits of a dog's intelligence. We would become much more tolerant if we were to compare its limits with those of a child who can walk, but not yet talk or understand spoken words. If a child of this age makes a mistake, we generally take the view that he or she is not old enough to understand the difference between right and wrong.

Imagine going to a foreign country where you could not speak the language, and asking someone to go to a particular shop in another town to buy a particular brand of perfume or after shave for you. It would be difficult but not impossible, because town names would be familiar and you could write down shop and brand names. Now imagine doing it without writing anything down and by just grunting instead of speaking. That's the level of communication we have with our dogs.

The biggest breakdown in our communication arises because invariably we are trying to get the dog to understand our values. This will never happen; after all, we have enough trouble trying to understand our own values without trying to inflict them upon another species. We, on the other hand, have the intelligence to learn about and understand canine values, and if we start to apply these to suit our own ends, communication between us becomes easier.

Let us take, for example, the fairly straightforward procedure of trying to teach our dog not to jump up on the settee.

Those of you who allowed it when your dog was a cuddly puppy, but decided at a later stage that you were going to stop it, will no doubt find that he will not get up on the settee while you are there, but you know that he does when you are not there. Quite often you will catch him getting off with a guilty look on his face when you enter the room. We take this look to mean he knows he should not have been there; in fact he knows that it is not good news to be there when you are around. When you are not around, the settee is warm and snug and being on it is self-rewarding. In fact, you taught him when he was a puppy just how comfortable the settee was, and the stroking and attention he received at the time reinforced this opinion. All he learned later was that the combination of you and him on the settee was bad news — not that getting on the settee was wrong. Puppies who were never allowed on the settee in the first place and, in your absence, were not allowed the access to find out how rewarding it was to be on there, never attempt to occupy it in later life.

Put simply, the learning process (as has been stated many times so far) involves the use of positive and negative reinforcement. That is the limit of the intelligence within our dogs — if they find it rewarding they will do it again. If they don't, they won't.

Question
We are thinking of getting a dog, but have never owned one before. We obviously want to get it trained and have been told that either German Shepherd Dogs or Border Collies are the most intelligent breeds. Is this true and would you advise us as first-time owners to get either one?

Answer
As an owner of both of these breeds at some time or another, I can certainly vouch for the fact that they are very trainable, although this is very different from intelligent, German Shepherds and Collies have been bred over the years specifically to work for man. The traits that make them good working dogs are the fact that they have stamina and look the part for the job that is required of them — the visual presence of the German Shepherd Dog for guarding and the colour schemes and famous collie eye for herding sheep. Both breeds are oblivious to weather conditions, are agile and eager to please. Their

ability to learn, however, is no different from many other breeds.

My experience of the two breeds leads me to describe them as workaholics, but this can create problems within a pet environment. Choosing a breed with a highly-developed working attitude is unfair on the dog unless you intend to put its talents to a regular and useful purpose. My German Shepherds have always been police-trained working dogs, as well as regular competitors in the sport of working trials. My Collie was trained for explosive detection which requires regular and stimulative ongoing training. A colleague of mine once calculated that a particular Collie, working sheep, in one day covered 75 miles. This was not just a feat of stamina, it also required concentration (it worked for 75 miles, not just covered that distance).

Before choosing your breed, it is important to think about your environment and life-style and ask yourself the question, will the breed of my choice be suitable for my way of life? This is a question that needs an honest answer; my records show that the problems that arise in these two breeds are predominantly because they are housed in totally inadequate environments. A dog that is bred to work and not allowed to express itself under control will express itself out of control and be branded as a problem dog.

J

Jealousy

This is an emotion that is peculiar to humans and, contrary to how it may seem, dogs are not affected in the same way. True, they often get their noses put out of joint by changes in the environment and react in strange ways which give the appearance of jealousy, but in fact it all has to to with how they perceive the pecking order.

A typical recent example involved a dog that had always been treated as a surrogate child by the owners, their own children having married and left home. The problems arose when their grandchild visited them, with the dog showing aggression whenever they cuddled the child or paid any attention to him at all. They assumed that the dog was jealous, and so they started to pay extra attention to the dog whenever the grandchild visited them. This only made matters worse, to the point that the dog now had to be shut out of the room because their daughter was naturally concerned for the child's safety.

In fact, the dog was used to all the attention being paid to him and perceived the grandchild as a threat to his rank because he appeared to be granted more favours on his territory. It was noticeable that whenever they took the dog to visit their daughter, it showed no aggression at all towards the child. This is the major difference between jealousy as a human emotion and what the dog appears to exhibit — with the dog it is almost always environmental. Giving the dog more attention whenever the child was around only reinforced the dog's opinion of his higher rank, so that he reacted more forcefully when they resumed their attention on the child. The owners found this concept hard to accept, because they could not differentiate between jealousy as an emotion and the cold logic of the pack instinct, that rank has its privileges. The problem was resolved when I told the owners to go home and make a terrific fuss of a cushion (cuddle it and kiss it). They did so and the dog attacked the cushion. The answer was to demote the dog.

This was done quite simply by taking into account the privileges that we can inadvertently grant to our dogs and which are described in Chapter 3. These were denied to the dog gradually over a period of about two weeks, which resulted in his becoming much more tolerant of the attention shown to their grandson.

Joggers
See Chase, p.95.

Jumping up
This is a problem that the majority of my clients report their dogs as being guilty of, but they do not see it as a major issue. They usually say that they can control it by holding on to the dog until he calms down, or they shut the dog out before they allow people into the house. By doing this they are negating one of the main uses of the dog in our modern society — that of guardian of our families. What better deterrent can there be for someone who knocks on your door with bad intent, than to be faced when it is opened with a dog sitting quietly under control alongside its owner?

The root of the problem usually goes right back to puppyhood, when owners and visitors tolerated the puppy's exuberant greetings. If you look back to Chapter 5, you will see in the section Jumping Up (p.46) that the basic instinct is a food-soliciting, greeting behaviour. This later changes to a dominant gesture, that of establishing rank by placing paws on top of the other animal. Whatever the reason why your dog jumps all over visitors, the bottom line is the fact that your dog is dictating their freedom of movement into, or around your house — and that should be your job.

Question
We have tried everything to stop our dog jumping up at visitors, all to no avail. We now simply shut him in another room but he goes beserk, barking and scratching at the door. How can we stop him?

Answer

Teach him to sit! A dog cannot jump up if his bum is on the floor. That might sound as if it is a flippant answer — it is not.

One of the mistakes that people make when trying to control a dog that jumps up at people is to make everything negative. Don't do that, bad dog! Get down! Stop it! Everything is geared towards telling the dog what not to do and people often forget to tell it what it should be doing instead. This is also one of the faults we fall into when we are raising our children, we become too negative in our approach.

The simplest solution is to apply the principles of the sound aversion therapy mentioned in the Appendix whenever the dog jumps up, but immediately to tell it to 'sit' and offer it a tit-bit to encourage it to do so. If the tit-bit is held out at arm's length, it is a pretty dumb dog that jumps past it. The calm greeting regime mentioned under Hyperactivity (p.142) will also help with this particular problem.

Juvenile

It is a fact that dogs go through a period of development similar to that which in people we classify as the 'juvenile delinquent' stage. In both people and dogs it is a sign that they are going through puberty, when the body is being bombarded with hormones which it finds pretty difficult to cope with. Dogs reach this stage around nine to fourteen months — equivalent to humans at the age of fourteen to twenty years approximately. Like humans, their behaviour sometimes becomes slightly irrational, and it is how we cope with this behaviour that can establish whether or not we end up with a well-balanced adult or not — dogs or humans.

The onset of puberty in dogs can result in a rise in aggression, usually in the male towards other males, sometimes in the female. It can also give rise to aggression towards owners because, just like humans at this stage of development, they are trying to establish their own identity. Recognising the fact that they are going through a transitional period is the first step towards coping with the problems that arise, and making sure that your dog knows its place within your mixed human/canine pack is of utmost importance during this time. Chapter 3 explains.

It is around this age that dogs alter their appearance. Many people describe it as a leggy or lanky stage, and again this can

My Great Dane attacks the coffee table.

be likened to how teenagers change in appearance. This means that on top of all the hormonal activity, the body also has to cope with the stresses of growth, and this in itself can have a tremendous influence on how they behave.

With teenage humans, we often take the view that they will grow out of it, and quite often they do. With dogs, however, allowing irrational and unacceptable behaviour to continue will have a learning effect on them which they will not grow out of — the behaviour will become established. We need to think carefully about how we handle the problem, bearing in mind that some of it is as a result of stresses beyond our control, so that we can take away any reward that the dog might receive from whatever it is doing, without punishing the dog if at all possible. Take, for instance, a dog that starts to show aggression towards other dogs. If we punish it every time it growls, we could teach the dog that the presence of another dog is a prelude to punishment, and so compound the problem. However, interrupting the aggression, using one of the sound aversion techniques (*see* Appendix) and giving the dog a reward for passive exposure to another dog, will have the desired learning effect.

Question
My dog has started to act very strangely indeed. He is a ten-month-old Great Dane called Henry and we have had him since he was seven weeks old. We recently bought a new three-piece suite which meant that we had to alter the furniture around slightly in the room. For some strange reason, Henry

has taken a dislike to the coffee table which has been there since he arrived. He suddenly attacked it, biting one of the legs, but now he backs away from it, growling and snarling, and no matter how much we try to coax him towards it he continues to be aggressive. Is there a reason why he is behaving like this and what can we do about it?

Answer
For a start, you should stop trying to coax him near it; this is only convincing him that there is something strange about the table. What you are describing is stress-related, more common in big dogs than little ones and resulting from the growth spurts that he is experiencing at this stage. It has also been called 'fear of familiar situations'. Objects that the dog has seen all its life, if moved to a different location, can become unrecognisable to the dog for what they are. The more fuss we make about it, the worse the problem becomes.

What you should do is ignore his barking and growling, move the table back to its original position and use it for whatever purpose you did before (eating sandwiches from, perhaps). You will notice that Henry will suddenly take on a look of 'Oh! that's what it is' and immediately settle down. You can then let him see you move it back to wherever you want to keep it and this he will accept. Above all, do not make any fuss about what you are doing and be slightly offhand about what he is doing.

L

Lead/leash training

After house-training, this is possibly the next, quite often traumatic, thing we try to teach our puppy — how to walk properly on a lead. Many dogs are not introduced to the restrictions of a lead until they are old enough to go out into the big wide world for the first time. When you consider that they are having to cope with all the strange new experiences, expecting them also to cope with the strange sensation of being restricted by the neck is very unfair on them. In general, they thrash about like fish out of water in their attempts to escape, and not only can this make them lead shy, it hardly builds confidence for going out at all. The section on socialisation (p. 192) will give some tips on how to get them to accept the world outside the security of their homes/dens, but in this section we are concerned with how to get them to accept the lead.

Lead training can start as soon as the puppy has settled into his new environment, but instead of just putting him on a lead and waiting for him to learn that there is no escape from it, there is no reason why he should not learn about the restrictions of a lead in a stress-free way.

Put his collar and leash on whilst someone else mixes his food. Hold him on the far side of the room and when his food is placed on the floor, lead him to it and keep it on whilst he eats. When one of the family is due home, put his collar and leash on and hold him away from the entrance. When the person arrives, lead the puppy over to greet them. In fact the collar and lead can become the prelude to all sorts of exciting situations, and by the time he is old enough to go out, he will be quite pleased to put it on and will have become accustomed to the strange feel of it.

Throughout this section I refer to the use of a collar and not a choke chain. My reasons are explained under Choke Chains (p. 102).

Question

My dog has a phobia about the lead. Instead of rushing to the door when I pick it up to take him for a walk, he runs and hides. It's not that he doesn't enjoy going out, in fact he loves it and is quite happy to follow me if I don't have a lead with me. The problem is that we live near a busy road and a lead is essential. Is there anything that I can do to overcome his fear? He's a ten-month-old Staffordshire Bull Terrier.

Answer

No doubt his phobia goes right back to the initial introduction, and who knows what happened to him at that time. If he struggled, he may have hurt himself and would naturally blame the lead for the pain because that was the thing on his mind at the time. The best thing to do is to throw the old lead away and replace it with an extending lead, or vice versa. It would also help for a short period to change from a collar to a body harness and start to take him out via a different door. By changing all the circumstances surrounding the preparation for going for a walk, you can start to desensitise him to whatever part of the procedure triggers off the fear response. Providing he enjoys his walk, the visual change of the lead, the environmental change to another area and the fact that you are not fastening something onto his collar will very quickly overcome the problem. Changes back to the usual procedure can then be done one at a time. (*See also* the question under Sensitivity, p. 191).

Licking

Why dogs lick is described in Chapter 5. Where the problem has reached a problematical or embarrassing stage, for example licking visitors to the house, it can usually be quickly cured by using either a taste deterrent or a quick, well-aimed squirt of water. How to use these forms of aversion is described in the Appendix (Other Aversion Methods).

M and N

Mounting
See M in Chapter 5.

Mouthing
See Biting, p. 84.

Nervousness
We always feel sorry for a nervous dog, whereas we rarely feel sorry for an aggressive dog, but sometimes the two go hand in hand. As described under Aggression (p. 68), dogs exhibit three defence reflexes, fight, flight or freeze, and nervous dogs are likely to display any one of these depending upon the situation that is facing them. If they feel cornered they will either freeze or attack — if it is the latter it would be classified as nervous aggression. In general, though, they would prefer to take flight, which is the passive defence reflex.

Unfortunately, we as owners can unwittingly encourage nervous behaviour through our desire to make the dog feel more confident. When we first recognise that our dog is feeling insecure, whether it is exhibiting a desire to run away or showing aggression because it feels threatened and cornered, we usually try to reassure it by soothing it by voice and by hand: 'There, there, shush, shush, good dog, there's nothing to be frightened about.' This is exactly how we would try to reassure a frightened child, often with good effect. The trouble is that dogs learn differently from children and they invariably regard our soothing tones and gentle caress as praise — That's a good dog, you're doing exactly what I want you to do! If it is another person who is making the dog afraid, he or she also recognises the dog's lack of confidence and stops doing whatever it was that triggered off the reaction. The dog therefore receives two rewards for its unwanted behaviour. Firstly, the person backs away, stands still or stops doing whatever frightened the dog. Secondly, the owner rewards the dog's behaviour through the attempts to calm and reassure. Obviously, we should not punish fearfulness, but we can be slightly offhand to ensure that the dog is not rewarded.

In some cases the problem might be inherited from one or other of the parents; even so, it is my experience that once the owners are made aware that the way they treat the dog is actually encouraging the wrong behaviour and stop the reward, the dogs usually improve.

Nervous dogs need space around them and so, even if they have a tendency to aggression, I find that increasing their freedom of movement by swapping the usual short restrictive lead for an extending lead helps them to put a little more distance between themselves and the object of their fear. Sometimes they just need an extra metre or so to feel more confident, and the owner still has the ability to control the dog. This is called their critical distance, something that all animals possess, including humans, and is perhaps better explained as 'personal space'.

Quite often, when dealing with a case of nervous aggression or fearfulness, I find that some short-term diet therapy can help (*see* Diet, p. 106). It would be wise to consult your vet for advice on what would be a suitable diet for your dog if you feel that this is an area which might help.

I have also found that nervous dogs respond well to homoeopathic or Bach remedies (*see* Bach remedies, p. 80). It is encouraging that more and more vets are showing an interest in this form of complementary medicine, as they are in behaviour therapy in general, and again, your vet should be able to advise you or refer you on to a colleague who can.

Question
We have a two-year-old Corgi bitch called Bess who is extremely nervous of small children. The problem is that our grandchildren (six years and four years) often come round to visit us. Bess is never aggressive towards them, she just runs and hides, and nothing that we do will persuade her to come and meet them. What do you suggest that we should do?

Answer

Provided you are confident that Bess will not be aggressive, my advice would be to do nothing. Dogs that are not socialised early with small children have difficulty in accepting their high-pitched voices and rapid movements and are initially a little wary of them. I wonder, though, whether there is more to it with Bess. If she lives alone with just the two of you, she has possibly learnt that she can keep your attention when your grandchildren are there by behaving in the way that she does. If she genuinely does not feel comfortable around them, she should not be forced or persuaded to interact with them. However, I suspect that if they visit you regularly she will have got used to their presence by now, and her behaviour has become a self-rewarding habit — whilst you are trying to persuade her to be sociable you are giving her the attention that you would normally be giving to the children.

During the next two or three visits, totally ignore her. If she wants to run and hide, let her. Give all your attention to the children and you will probably find that she will try some other behaviour (like whining) to try to divert you back to her. This will confirm my suspicions that her nervousness is in fact, learned attention-seeking. If this is the case, for a few hours prior to the arrival of the children, ignore Bess. When the children arrive, all of you take Bess for a walk — still not trying to get her to interact with them, but leaving her to make the first move. If this regime is kept up over the next few visits, I think you will find that Bess will start to view the arrival of your grandchildren as a prelude to a pleasant experience. You can then change the pleasurable experiences by, one day, withholding her food until the children arrive and allowing them to feed her — or perhaps withholding all tit-bits until the children arrive. Ideally, provided you have first established that her nervousness is really attention-seeking and not a genuine fear, you can resort to a technique called 'flooding'. Get the children to stay with you for a few days and let them be responsible (under supervision) for everything that is important to Bess — even to the point that it is one of them who allows her out into the garden.

Neutering
See Castration (dogs), p. 92; Spaying (bitches), p. 194.

Obedience classes

It is the responsibility of all dog owners to ensure that their dogs are properly trained, and for most people this will involve them attending their local dog-training classes for at least one course of lessons. But be warned! Although this is not meant to be a criticism of training classes in general, it is a fact of life that there are some good and a lot of bad clubs around.

After many, many years during which dog-training techniques remained in the doldrums, over the last few years especially great strides forward have been made and more positive reward-based methods of training are being employed, instead of the old-fashioned punishment-orientated negative approach. Some clubs, however, refuse to move with the times and continue to advise owners that, if their dogs do something wrong, they should be punished as a way of teaching them not to do the same thing again. This method, properly applied by an expert trainer, can in some cases prove to be successful. But the average pet owner is not an expert — if they were, there would be no need to attend classes in the first place. In general, the punishment for the deed is applied too late and all the dog learns is to avoid the punishment, not to stop the act that earned it. This is evident in a lot of clubs where, for example, a dog is seen to lunge towards another dog and then immediately show submission to its owner. What the dog has learnt is that when its owner is standing next to it and another dog approaches, the owner is going to get cross; it is good canine insurance, therefore, to chase the other dog away before the owner sees it. It has certainly not learnt that the act of lunging is what it has been punished for, because if it had, it would not have done it.

Alternatively, a more forward-thinking club, instead of advising the owner to watch for the first sign of aggression and punish the dog, would tell the owner to reward all passive exposure to another dog. This would be done by bringing another dog into sight, but at a reasonable distance, and, provided there was no sign of aggression, rewarding the dog and then removing the other one from the scene.

Gradually the distance can be reduced until the dog understands that the presence of another dog is a prelude to reward and not to punishment. Withholding the reward when the dog lunges becomes the punishment. This technique is called systematic desensitisation, but I call it common sense.

Obviously, this cannot be done in a classroom situation, but if the dog is being disruptive it is not learning anything, and neither are the rest of the dogs in the class. Until the problem dog is calm in the presence of other dogs, for everyone's sake it should not be in that sort of environment. A good club would start the desensitisation programme before or after the main lesson and gradually integrate the dog back into the class. A good club would make sure that the number of dogs in each class was kept to a manageable minimum, so that each owner could get his or her fair share of personal attention and the dogs would not feel crowded and therefore defensive. Clubs that have large classes of twenty or more, with only one instructor on the floor, should be avoided, because very little 'one-to-one' attention can be given and if it is, it will be to the detriment of the rest of the class. I realise that smaller classes will cost more per lesson, but I believe that the days of large noisy classes at 50p a night, which operate a 'join in at any time' system, should be a thing of the past. The way forward is through small, structured classes — around ten is ideal — all starting at the same time for a course of eight to twelve lessons. This not only allows for individual attention, but also creates a class camaraderie and, with it, a more social environment.

The thing to do is to go and watch a lesson or two without taking the dog. If you like what you see and you think the dogs and owners are learning — fine. If you don't like what you see, look elsewhere.

Question

I have been attending training classes with my eighteen-month-old Pointer since he was six months old. In the class he is the star pupil and he has won a lot of the club competitions which are held regularly. However, outside the class he is still extremely disobedient. He pulls on the lead, he won't come back when I call him and he is terrible with visitors to the house — he just won't leave them alone.

He just wants to be friendly, but I know that not everyone likes dogs. If I shut him in another room he barks like mad and scratches the door. Why won't he behave himself outside the class, the way he does inside?

Answer
Teaching a dog what you mean by certain words of command is only part of the training process. As a direct descendant of the wolf, the dog retains a very strong pack instinct and, in a pack, rank has its privileges. If, at home, you are allowing your dog the privileges of high rank, then he will see you as the underdog and someone who has no right to tell him what to do. This is the same in any species that operates a hierarchical rank structure. Allowing your dog to precede you through doorways, passageways or gateways; allowing him to occupy your bed and chairs but respecting his sleeping areas as his alone; feeding him before you eat; allowing him to beg food from your table — all these are privileges of rank. By inadvertently promoting your dog, you lose the right to lead and control. He may obey you in the dog club, but within that environment he has no other choice. If, however, when the instructor opens the door at the end of the lesson, your dog pulls you out, you have just allowed him to regain the rank that you have tried to take off him in the lesson.

Rank also has responsibilities and among these are that he should lead the pack — that's why he still pulls on the lead, it is his job to be out in front; to keep the pack together — that's why he will not come back to you when you call, it is not your job; to defend the den — that's why he is so troublesome with your visitors, he is not being friendly, he is making sure that they move about on his terms but in a passive and not an aggressive way. What right do you have to isolate a higher ranking animal, especially when there are intruders in his den? That's why he complains so much when you try to do so. None of these problems has anything to do with training, they are all to do with attitude. If you get the attitude right and your dog sees you as the leader, all your previous training will pay dividends. If you make sure that the privileges of rank are yours, everything else will slot into place. (*See also* Dominance (p. 110); Pulling (p. 167.)

P

Play/possession

Dogs learn through play and the reward that their games give them. The games that puppies play are all designed to teach them the skills required for hunting and killing (see Chapter 5, section C). Stalking, pouncing and play biting with their litter brothers and sisters are all hunting games. They also play competitive games of rough-and-tumble and tug-of-war, and these are dominance games. The winner of a tug-of-war game is the one who eventually ends up with the tug toy, be it a stick or a sock. Invariably, they will take it back to their bed or to a favourite corner of the room or garden. Sometimes they will hide under the coffee table or your bed, thus creating a den atmosphere where they can trophy and possess their prize. The more possessions they win, the higher ranking they think they are. It is a fact that dogs which have lots of toys that are freely available to them in the house are very possessive about the house, especially where visitors are concerned. Dogs that have lots of toys in the garden are very possessive about the garden, but less so in the house. The area where they are allowed to accumulate their possessions becomes the area where they exhibit dominant attitudes. That is not to say that every dog will follow this pattern. Some dogs have lots of toys and never cause any trouble, but with those that do, the area where their behaviour is at its worst will always be the area where they hoard their trophies.

Ideally, dogs that have a predisposition towards dominance-related problems should never be allowed to win any competitive games over their owners. A good maxim would be: if you don't think you are going to win, don't play; dogs have different values from those of humans, and our sporting attitude of 'it's not the winning, it's the taking part' would be laughed at by the whole of the canine species — dogs only play to win.

Many of my clients are of the mistaken belief that they usually win these tug-of-war or strength games. When I ask them what they do with the tug toy after they have managed to get it out of the dog's mouth, they invariably tell me that they throw it for the dog, or drop it on the floor. When I say, 'So the dog ends up with the toy after all,' they realise that it is the one who takes home the trophy that has won the competition.

Dispossessing dominant dogs of all their toys except one, and taking control of this toy yourself so that they can only play with it when you decide to play, and making sure that you always win the game and keep possession of the toy, is a good way of demoting the dog and promoting yourself. It should always be borne in mind that whereas humans play games to amuse themselves, dogs don't. If they play a shake-the-rag game on their own, they are practising their killing technique. If they play a tug-the-rag game with you, they are testing your strength and trying to promote their rank by winning and KEEPING the rag.

Question

I am beginning to think that my dog is a kleptomaniac. Although he has lots of his own toys he rarely plays with them, but he will insist of stealing my things. Socks, gloves, purse, underwear — as soon as I put down anything that he can pick up, he does. If I try to take it off him he growls at me and clamps his teeth down harder on whatever he has in his mouth. The only way I can get it back is to wait until he takes it to his bed and then I distract him with a tit-bit, whilst someone else gets the article back. Why does he do it and how can I stop him?

Answer

He is doing it as a statement of his rank, and before we examine how best to stop him, we should examine why he chooses to take your possessions, when he has so many of his own. First of all, it is the fact that he has so many of his own that gives him the impression that he has the right to everything else. He has probably learnt that if he picks up one of his own toys, nobody takes any notice of him — toys are only toys to dogs if someone else joins in the challenge for them.

However, as soon as he picks up something of value, every-one joins in the challenge. If he trophies an article of yours and you try to take it off him, he will growl to get you to back down, which you would be sensible to do at this stage because dogs can move their mouths four times faster than we can move our hands. His 'kleptomania', as you call it, was learned the first time he picked up something of value that belonged to you — you reacted immediately and took part in the dominance game that he had initiated. Probably, just prior to this, he had tried to get you to join in a tussle for one of his own toys and you were too busy to take any notice. The more of these games that he wins the more aggressive he will become whilst playing them — and there is of course the added reward of a tit-bit after he has won the article.

What you need to do is reverse the roles. Take away all his toys — not as a challenge, do it when he is not there. The fact that he does not have a variety of possessions scattered around as a visual display of his rank is the first stage in overcoming the problem. One of these toys should be selected by you as a reward for him doing the things that you want him to do. A light trailing house line should be attached to his collar, so that instead of taking things off him, you can gently take him away from things. In this way, if after he has earned the toy he tries to keep it, you can repossess it until the next time you want to reward him with it again. For a few days, selected items should be left in strategic places and suitably booby trapped with a taste or a sound deterrent (*see* Appendix, Other Aversion Methods). Every time he tries to take one of these items, he will find it unpleasant and spit it out. You should gently pull him away from it with the line and take possession yourself. The result of this will be that every challenge that he lays down you will win. The more you win, the less he will want to challenge you and his kleptomania will be overcome. This procedure should be done in conjunction with an overall rank reduction programme and Chapter 3 describes the areas that can be worked on to do this.

Pulling

Although pulling on the lead is generally considered to be a training problem, it is interesting to note that when I reviewed my figures for the last year, pulling on the lead came out as the most complained-about problem. Not that it was the reason why the owners consulted me, it was reported as a secondary problem and nearly always exhibited by dogs that had dominant attitudes and related behaviour problems. In the section on Obedience classes (p. 161) the question and answer is a classic example of this.

It is my experience that stopping a dog pulling does not reduce its dominant attitude. However, reducing the dominance does stop the pulling. The instinct of the dog dictates that it should not walk ahead of a more dominant animal, and the same is true of humans. When you consider that over 50 per cent of the clients that I see have attended a training class, where learning to walk to heel is the first thing that is usually tackled and the most practised exercise, why should it come out as the most common problem exhibited by dominant dogs? The answer is simple — learning what the word heel means does not necessarily mean that the dog has to obey it if he does not recognise the owner as the leader.

It is obvious, though, that reducing the dog's status within the home by recognising and transferring all privileges away from the dog and on to the owner (*see* Chapter 3) will be of no use if the dog is allowed to walk in front of the owner when out for a walk. The simple act of leading instead of being led will reinstate the dog's idea of his rank. To this end, some time ago I researched and developed a combined collar and leash called the Col-leash (*see* Appendix). I have found this a terrific aid, when combined with an overall rank reduction programme, because it allows the dog to walk naturally and display normal canine body postures, but makes it impossible for it to pull.

Question

My Burnese Mountain Dog is very strong — and I'm not! Despite training, he still pulls on a lead and if he decides to go somewhere, he goes, and drags me with him. Not only is it no pleasure taking him out, I realise just how dangerous it is.

I have tried the various head collars that are available, but he struggles so much that he makes his nose red raw. Is there anything else that you can suggest?

Answer

Dogs that object to any form of physical control are usually quite dominant characters and it would be wise for you to look at your daily routine with the dog and establish whether you are in fact encouraging his attitude that he should lead. Chapter 3 will show you some of the areas that need to be worked upon to change his attitude. Incidentally, the Col-leash (*see*

Appendix) tends to have a very high acceptance rate with dogs that object to other forms of head collar and the main distributors will fit one on your dog first to make sure that it is suitable. But if your dog objects to any form of physical control, there is a different approach that can be used which does not require any strength.

Many dogs respond quite well to a technique which involves the use of a Flexi Leash (brand name). But before I describe this technique, we need to understand just what is happening with a pulling dog. As soon as the lead is tightened, the dog has something to strain against. The fact that pressure invites counter-pressure is a well-known principle, easily understood if you think what your initial reaction would be if someone grabbed your sleeve and started to pull you towards them. Most people would resist and pull away — it's called negative thigmotaxis if you want the posh name for it. By using a Flexi Leash without applying the brake, there is nothing to pull against — all the dog is able to do is walk faster than you. By pulling back on the handle of the leash and partly applying the brake, the brake runs over the top of the ratchet causing the end of the leash to judder. This juddering action transfers to the front end of the dog, making the legs wobble and interrupting the dog's stride. As soon as the forward motion has been stopped in this way the brake should be released again. Three or four repetitions of this quickly teach the dog:

1 There is nothing to pull against.
2 Every time he tries to walk faster than you, his legs do a little dance, which makes it impossible.

This is a technique that needs some practice, preferably by fastening the end of the lead onto something solid at home first, before you apply it to the dog. If the Col-leash does not do the job, the same distributors will demonstrate this technique as well.

Punishment

Punishment as a training aid just does not work. However, until fairly recently, this was the way that dogs were traditionally trained (*see* Compulsion, p. 103). The danger of using punishment is that the dog might learn the wrong thing. The example given under Obedience classes (p. 161), of the dog that lunges out at other dogs, shows the difference between a punishment-orientated training programme and a positive reinforcement programme. As has been stated many times so far, dogs learn through reward, and even then the reward has to coincide with the act, or within two seconds of the act, for it to have a learning effect.

Most of the people to whom I talk readily agree with this principle, and this is all very well when it comes to theory. However, human nature is such that we are in fact a punishment-orientated animal, and when I pose the following theoretical scenario, it proves to most people just how readily we will resort to this form of training.

> Suppose your dog was loose in the park and, from a distance of fifty yards, you saw it bark at a mother with her child and then rush in and bite the child. You screamed, 'COME HERE, Fido!' and he returned to you immediately. Would you tell him he was a good boy?

In reality not many people would, they would probably hit the dog. But this would be to teach it that the act before its last one was not good. Its last act was to obey your recall command and, from the dog's point of view, that is what it is being punished for.

If you made a terrific fuss of the dog for returning, the mother would tell the police that you praised the dog for biting her child.

If you went on to explain to the police that you were praising the dog for coming when called, they would find it pretty hard to accept and so would the judge.

The problem is that humans cannot separate values from straightforward learning procedures. Dogs and other animals rely purely on instinct. If, for instance, the dog felt threatened by the mother and child and attacked the weaker of the two as a form of defence, that would be normal (although unacceptable) dog behaviour — remember, dogs bite. Returning to the security of its owner when called, only to receive punishment for returning, would simply make it wary of obeying in the future, not teach it that it should not bite children. Its aggressive behaviour should be dealt with as a separate issue. From this example, it can be seen that instead of looking at what we are really teaching the dog, we are clouding the whole issue with human values and creating confusion. We are usually too ready to punish the dog for what is wrong, instead of concentrating on and rewarding what is right, but does the dog understand what we are trying to teach it at all?

If punishment is used as a first-time training aid and the dog learns the wrong thing, not only do we create confusion, we also create mistrust. Where punishment, in the name of training, is invariably used is described under House-training (p. 140).

Puppies

When choosing a puppy, especially if you are a first-time owner, there are some golden rules which, if you follow them, will pay tremendous dividends in the long term. Recently, with TV personality Katie Boyle, I recorded an audio cassette tape called 'Think Dog'. This is a tape that is designed to give owners advice on choosing, bringing home and settling in a new puppy. It is available with an accompanying booklet, which has been illustrated by William Rushton, from Our Dogs Publishing Co. Ltd., Oxford Road, Station Approach, Manchester M60 1SX.

My last book, also called *Think Dog*, goes into great depth about choosing a puppy and the critical periods of development that they go through (H. F. & G. Witherby, 14 Henrietta Street, London WC2E 8QJ). Briefly, the rules to bear in mind are as follows:

1   Before deciding on the breed, find out all about it: exercise needs, size and coat type, inherent instincts, and ask yourself — will this type of dog suit my domestic circumstances?

2   Always go to a breeder who will show you the puppies with the mother. Be wary if the mother is not available for whatever reason. It could be because her temperament is not good, or it could be that the 'breeder' is in fact a 'dealer', and the puppies were born elsewhere (I shall discuss puppy farms and the like overleaf).

3   If it is just a family pet that you want, don't necessarily pick the puppy that rushes out to greet you. This could be the most dominant of the litter and if IT CHOOSES YOU, this might the first of many other decisions it will make. Don't feel sorry for and choose the quiet one that stays out of your way and is ignored by the rest of

the pups. This might grow up to be very nervous and too submissive for family life. You need to choose one that is fairly confident without being too pushy.

4 Arrange with the breeder to collect the puppy when it is between seven and nine weeks old. Up to seven weeks is known as the canine socialisation period, during which time puppies learn how to be dogs. It is vitally important that they spend this time with their mother, litter brothers and sisters. From seven to fourteen weeks is known as the human socialisation period, during which time they learn how to be dogs within a domestic environment. Each week that goes by up to fourteen weeks, they are missing out on this essential socialisation and becoming too attached to other dogs. After fourteen weeks, unless they have been raised in a busy 'mad-house' with lots of visitors and normal domestic stimuli, they could suffer from a condition known as kennelosis. These dogs never really bond with people and, although they will live with us, their great joy in life is other dogs and they become the type of dog that we would prefer not to have as a pet.

For more information, see Socialise (p. 192).

Now back to the puppy farms that I mentioned earlier. Puppy farmers are just what the name implies — people who breed dogs purely for profit. Many of these puppies are kept in appalling conditions — old caravans, old cars, draughty outhouses and barns. The bitches that produce these litters are taken away from their puppies, sometimes when the latter are only four weeks old, simply to get them fit enough to produce another litter when they next come into season. The puppies are loaded into crates, often cramped and with inadequate food and water, and driven along the motorways to pick-up points where they are handed over to dealers. From there they are sold to unsuspecting pet homes, who generally find that within a few days the puppy becomes ill — usually with severe gastro-intestinal problems. By that time the family have become attached to the puppy and pay out for week after week to get it well again. Many of the puppies are sold with very impressive-looking pedigree forms, but these are often false, since anyone can obtain a pedigree form and, with the help of a dog book, copy out a line of ancestors.

The network of dealers is highly organised and, on the face of it, they are very caring people. But when they only pay between £25 and £35 per puppy and sell them with these 'Mickey Mouse' pedigrees for £250 to £300, it makes sense to develop the right image so that this highly lucrative trade can continue.

There are many organisations now trying to put a stop to this loathsome trade, but it is very difficult. For a start, many of the farmers do not hold breeding licences, and the ironic thing is that, at the time of writing, the local authorities are only empowered to enter and inspect licensed premises. There is one way of stopping them and that is through education of the pet-owning public. If everyone who wanted to buy a puppy insisted on seeing the mother with her litter, and made local and veterinary inquiries about the breeder if the mother was not available — sometimes there are genuine reasons — then very shortly there would be no retail outlet and the farmers would be out of business.

Rank reversal

Throughout this book I have made mention of owners inadvertently raising the rank of their dogs to the point where the dogs have become a problem because the owner has lost the right to give commands. Chapter 3 has been constantly referred to because, in general, the way that we live with our dogs today is usually the root cause of this problem. In order to reduce the dog's view of its rank within our canine/human pack, we need to establish certain rules. The following are not placed in any particular order, because one is as important as the other. Neither is it that important that every rule is established; in most cases, by making a specific effort on just a few, the dog changes its viewpoint about its role within your household. These rules can be laid down one at a time and, in this way, confrontation is avoided. It may take two or three days to establish the first rule that you decide upon, for example pushing through doorways, but you should persevere until this is well and truly understood before moving on to the next stage. As each rule is understood by the dog, the next becomes easier to establish.

1 Make sure that you are the one who goes first through doorways and narrow openings. The simplest way of achieving this is to close all doors in the house for a few days so that the dog's freedom of movement becomes dependent upon the doors that you choose to allow him through. Don't tell him to stay, sit, or wait — this is basically asking him if he minds if you go first. Ideally, he should grant you the right of rank by allowing you to precede him. If he tries to barge in front of you, slam the door shut — be careful not to trap his nose. Initially, you may have to repeat this procedure four or five times at each

Rank reversal

door, but he will quickly get the message that when you open a door, he steps backwards.

2   Make sure that he does not occupy your beds or chairs. Many of my clients tell me that their dog is not allowed on furniture, but not being allowed is different from not even trying. You, however should be able to occupy the areas where your dog generally chooses to sleep. Besides his bed, there will be many other places around the house and you should spend a day or so mapping these out — you will be surprised how many there are. Deny him access to some and make a point of occupying the others.

3   Make sure you eat before he does. Either change his meal-times to follow yours, or mix up his food in his presence and then make a point of sitting down and eating a biscuit. By going through the act of eating first, you are stating to your dog that at feeding time, the highest ranking eats first and therefore gets the richest pickings.

4   Do not allow him to occupy key areas in the house. Busy doorways, main entrances, top steps are all areas that

would be controlled by the Alpha (highest ranking) figure. Making these areas inaccessible is the easiest solution, and although physical barriers might get in your way for a few days, it will be worth it in the long run.

5   Make sure that when you want to go from A to B you do so by the shortest route — in other words, make the dog move out of your way, even if he appears to be asleep. Making him wear a light trailing house line attached to his collar so that you can gently pull him to one side makes the point very clearly that lower ranks step aside for higher ranks.

6   Make certain rooms in the house off-limits altogether, especially your bedroom. Your dog should learn that although you have access to the whole of the den, he is only allowed in part of it.

7   Do not allow him to demand attention. Dogs learn to do this in a variety of ways: nudging your arm for a stroke, pretending they need to go into the garden, especially when you are on the phone. All privileges should be earned first, even if it is only complying with a command to sit. All his attempts to initiate some sort of interaction between you should be put onto your terms.

8   Having earned the privilege of being stroked, you should only stroke him on his head, neck and shoulders. These are the dominant regions of the dog and careful observation in the park of two high-ranking dogs will show you that the most dominant will place his chin or a paw on the neck and withers of the other dog.
    Do not fall for the trick of a paw being placed on your arm in an attempt to get you to rub his chest instead, or for the trick of lying on his back for the same purpose. In the wild, the only way that a dominant dog would experience this sensation would be when he was on the back of a bitch (*see* Chapter 5, M. Mounting).

9   Remove all his toys and possession. Select one of these and keep it under your control. He should only be allowed to play with this toy when you want him to and even then he should earn it first by obeying a command of some sort.

Do not allow him to keep it afterwards, take it off him again until you want him to play with it again.

10 Only allow him five minutes to eat his food. Dominant dogs have a habit of leaving some or all of their food for long periods of time, almost as a visual display of their rank — this is my food and I know that no one else will eat it. Even if he starts to eat it after four-and-a-half minutes, it should be taken up after five.

11 Make sure that he greets you first thing in the morning and not the other way round. It is surprising how many of my clients, who have dominant dogs, do this every morning without realising. It is the lower ranks that approach the higher ranks to greet them.

12 Increasing your control through regular obedience sessions, even if they only last five or ten minutes a day, will help tremendously. These sessions should be done on a lead and collar so that you are in the position of being able to insist that the dog obeys.

Recall

This is probably one of the most difficult problems to overcome because, from the dog's point of view, not coming is more rewarding than coming. If the dog does not obey, the walk is extended, if he does obey, the walk is stopped and he is taken home. Ultimately, the responsibility of keeping the pack together should lie with the pack leader, and if the dog is ignoring the owner's commands to return, the owner should look at his relationship with the dog in general.

Whenever an owner complains about his dog's failure to return when called, I usually ask how readily the dog responds in the house or garden. Generally he tells me that he has no trouble, but after he has been in my office for about ten minutes and I ask him to call the dog over to him, it usually takes three or four calls before the dog obeys. I am not suggesting that owners like this have told me a lie about the dog's readiness to respond at home, it is just that it has not created a problem and therefore they have not noticed. At the end of the day, if the owners have to keep repeating the recall command to the dog in the confines of their own home, they can hardly expect the dog to obey them when they are out in the park with all the added distractions of different smells and other dogs. Obviously, they should first improve their recall in the home and garden before the dog is allowed off the lead in wide open spaces.

Assuming this has been done, the first few sessions should be carried out in a fairly enclosed area, with the dog trailing a light line. One command only should be given, and if the dog does not immediately respond, the line should be tugged — not as a correction, only to reinforce the command. It is a good idea to feed the dog only after it has had its run and, if the dog is only fed once a day, changing to two or three smaller meals, with each portion following his exercise, will increase the incentive to return. Failing this, taking the portion of his daily food ration to the park should do the trick.

Once the recall response has been improved, the owner should get into the habit of calling the dog three or four times during each walk. Praise the dog and give a tit-bit or play with a toy and then allow him to run off again. This will overcome the dog's idea that being called is a prelude to going home.

Question
We have tried every possible way to teach our dog to come back to us when he is called, but to no avail. We have never hit him, he has been castrated, we have had him on a long line, we have taken food to the park, he has been to training classes — you name it and we have tried it. Unless you know another method. Can you help, PLEASE?

Answer
There is a method which has proved to be successful in the past and its effectiveness is thanks to a Russian scientist called Pavlov. You may be aware of the research that he did into conditioned reflexes, but if not, one of the experiments that he conducted was on the dog's salivatory rate. He proved that, by ringing a bell and then blowing meat powder into the dog's mouth, he could quickly get the dog to salivate when he rang the bell on its own. What has this got to do with the recall? Simply that a conditioned reflex is something that the dog has no control over; therefore if you can teach your dog to salivate when it hears a certain sound, you are more than halfway towards curing your recall problem. If the dog is salivating, it will need to satisfy the physiological urge that has been trig-

gered off. If you have some juicy tit-bits with you, it's a dumb dog that will run in the opposite direction.

Buy yourself a whistle — any whistle will do providing the dog has not heard that tone before. Whenever you want to, give your dog a tit-bit, and I would arrange that part of his daily food ration is given in the form of tit-bits so that they can be given a dozen or so times a day. Prior to giving him one, blow the whistle, but do not say anything. Do the same when you feed him the remains of his food. If you continue this regime for a few days, you will notice that the whistle will produce the same results that Pavlov achieved. You can then start to blow the whistle when your dog is in the garden and you are in the house. By the time he comes through the door, he should be well and truly drooling. This unpredictable regime of whistle, salivate, tit-bit/daily food ration should be continued until the recall itself becomes a conditioned reflex. Once you stop the tit-bits, the salivation at the sound of the whistle will quickly extinguish. This is an entirely different method from 'positive reinforcement' which will be discussed next.

Reinforcement

There are two kinds of reinforcement: positive and negative. A positive reinforcement is anything which, occurring in conjunction with an act, tends to increase the probability that the act will occur again.

A negative reinforcement is something the subject wants to avoid. Training any animal to perform a particular act is possible using these two aids, and that includes humans. Training a behaviour, whether it is to get a dog to jump an obstacle, or to potty-train a child, is best achieved if there are no negative circumstances involved.

Unfortunately, new dog training books are still being published that advocate Neanderthal training methods. One of my students, on a correspondence course in canine behaviour that I wrote and tutor for the Animal Care College and Canine Studies Institute (Ascot House, High Street, Ascot, Berkshire SL5 7JG), reviewed a book that was published recently. In it, the authors state that the best way to settle a puppy in at night is as follows:

If he howls, shake the hell out of him, ensuring that you do not snap his neck back. Should this fail, the fault is yours for not using the correct level of anger. The object of the exercise being to frighten not to hurt.

My student went on to say, 'I dread to think of the state of mind of a sensitive puppy that has been subjected to this treatment'.

Karen Pryor, an American authority on marine-mammal behaviour, said: 'Punishment is humanity's favourite method. When the behaviour goes wrong, we think first of punishment. Scold the child, spank the dog, dock the paycheck, fine the company, torture the dissident, invade the country, and so on.' The problem is that when we find out that the punishment does not stop the behaviour, what do we do? WE ESCALATE THE PUNISHMENT.

To a certain extent, punishment after the act can have a learning effect on humans, but that is because we have the power of logical thought patterns — *I am in gaol now for a crime that I committed last year. I do not like being in jail, so I will commit no more crimes.* Other animals do not have this ability, therefore punishing unwanted behaviour after the act only confuses them. Sometimes even punishment during the act can have the reverse effect from one we are trying to achieve.

Question

My two-year-old German Shepherd Dog is very aggressive towards all dogs when he is with me. It doesn't matter whether it is a dog or a bitch, a puppy or an adult; as soon as he sees them he flies out at them. If I spot the dog first, I give him a sharp check on his choke chain to bring him to heel, about turn him and walk in the other direction. If he spots it first, he often takes me by surprise and, even though I am a big-built man, he has pulled me off my feet on more than a few occasions. I have sent him away for training and when I collected him he was running loose in a compound with four or five other dogs with no trouble at all. The trainer said that his kennel maid used to walk him on the lead through the local town and he was no trouble when they met another dog. None of the dog club instructors who have walked him have ever experienced any problems. My vet has castrated him, but that has made no difference at all. Do you think he is being over-protective towards me and, if so, what can I do about it?

Answer

There may be an element of protective behaviour involved and it would be as well for you to refer to the rank reversal procedures outlined on pp. 174–7 to ensure that your dog sees you as the protector of the territory. But I am more inclined to think that the way you have been handling the situation has had the greatest influence upon your dog's aggressive behaviour. The fact that it is non-selective aggression (all dogs, regardless of status); the fact that he will run free with other dogs; the fact that he does not behave aggressively with other people would all point to the fact that he is not an aggressive dog by nature. Therefore, the behaviour must be learned and the common denominator is you.

If you think it through from the dog's point of view, whenever a dog appears on the horizon, you give him a sharp, and possibly painful tug on the chain and head off in the other direction. Now that would not have happened if the other dog had not appeared, therefore it must be the other dog's fault. The presence of another dog has become a prelude to him getting punished. I know what I would do if I were your dog: I would try to chase off the other dog before you saw it. When other people have got hold of his lead, he has not been punished and so there was no need to show aggression.

I can understand the fact that once a dog starts to become aggressive the owner starts to lose confidence and, as a result, starts to overreact. But it is this overreaction that creates a vicious circle and compounds the problem. There are two problems to overcome:

1   To increase your confidence.
2   To change your dog's expectations about what the presence of another dog means and therefore reduce the aggression.

This should be done in the following way:

a)   Change the choke chain to a broad leather collar so that there is no pain-associated element involved.
b)   Change the short restrictive lead to a strong Flexi Leash. This will increase your dog's freedom of movement, and that in itself will have a calming effect.
c)   Temporarily, fit him with a soft muzzle (Mikki Muzzles

are ideal and obtainable from most pet shops). This is to ensure that there can be no damage if he does take you by surprise, but it is primarily designed to increase your confidence. This type of muzzle is designed to restrict the movement of the dog's jaws, making biting imposs- ible but allowing you to feed the dog, which is the next stage. (Do not leave it on too long in hot weather!)

d) If he usually gets three walks a day, make sure that you split his daily food ration into three equal portions. These should be further split into three or four smaller portions and put into plastic bags to be taken with you on a walk. For the next week or so, your dog will only get fed when out walking, with a portion being given after he meets another dog.

The procedure will be as follows. When you see another dog, be prepared for him to lunge out, which he surely will out of habit. Do not apply the brake on the Flexi until he does, so that you do not transmit your tension to him. Stop him if he does lunge — the collar will ensure that he will not feel any pain — but do not say anything negative. Gently call him back to you and take a portion of food from your pocket. Let him have that portion and continue with the walk. Repeat the procedure until he has had a third of his daily food ration and then go home. Keep a portion in hand in case you meet a dog.

Although this may sound as if you will be giving him a reward for lunging out at other dogs, in fact it will have the reverse effect. Because he will not be punished, either physi- cally or verbally, when another dog appears, he will begin to view other dogs as a prelude to being fed. When you reach the stage when he looks at you when another dog appears, you can dispense with the muzzle. Quite soon, the food reward can be replaced with the occasional tit-bit, or a game with his favourite toy, or just some verbal praise.

Rescue dogs

Some of what follows may be a duplicate of information con- tained elsewhere in the book. The reason for this is that I want to treat the subject of re-homing rescue dogs as a complete and independent section. Sadly, there are thousands of dogs in rescue centres around the country, waiting for someone to give them a home. On a daily basis, there are people who are pre-

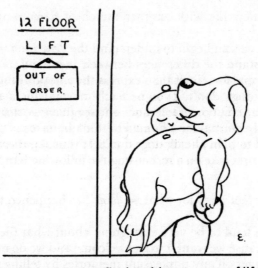

12 FLOOR

LIFT

OUT OF ORDER.

Choose a dog that fits in with your way of life.

pared to take on one of these dogs rather than buying a puppy, but rescuing a dog is not always an easy task if the new owner is not aware of some of the pitfalls. To make it easier for these people to understand their new dog better, I intend to condense a lot of what has been written elsewhere under this one heading.

Everyone feels sorry for a rescued dog, and in the absence of any information about its previous home we immediately assume that it was found walking down the M1 motorway where it had been thrown out of a car; rescued from a garden shed where it had been locked in and almost starved to death; or taken off a cruel family who used to beat it up every morning just in case it did anything wrong that day. Unfortunately, there are numbers of dogs that have experienced this sort of cruelty, but the majority that pass through the caring hands of the various animal shelters are being re-homed for perfectly genuine reasons.

The purpose of this section is to help you to understand your dog and to get you to realise that up until today, everything that has happened to your dog is history. What is important to the dog now is the future.

Certainly, under certain circumstances, previous unpleasant experiences might affect your dog's behaviour, but at this stage we need to understand the dog as an individual and how it will view its new life with another bunch of hard-to-understand humans.

Before we can begin to understand the dog, we must first try to understand the differences between them and us. It is perfectly normal for a human to express the emotion of sorrow and concern; dogs don't. It is perfectly normal for a human to express the emotion of tolerance and forgiveness; dogs don't. It is perfectly normal for a human to think in terms of time structures and to plan ahead; dogs don't. It is usual, therefore, that when we first take on a rescue dog the following happens:

1   We feel sorry for what we *think* has happened to it in the past.
2   We tend to be very easy-going about what the dog does because we want it to feel welcome and we do not want to trigger off any unpleasant memories by telling it off until it has settled in.
3   We make plans to train the dog later, once it has settled in.

Dogs live for NOW. They don't lie there thinking about what life used to be like. Memories of former experiences are only triggered off by familiar audio, visual or chemical reminders. A familiar voice can produce excitement or fear, as can a familiar shape such as a rolled-up newspaper or a stick held in a particular way. Certain smells, like creosote, can trigger off a fear of being locked in a shed, but until these problems manifest themselves, to the dog, out of sight, sound or smell is out of mind.

We have a rescue Jack Russell which is typical of the breed; the only time she shows real aggression is if we fold up a newspaper and then she turns into the incredible hulk. Obviously, her previous owner used a rolled-up newspaper to discipline her, a stupid, ineffective 'old wives' tale' way of training dogs. Consequently, because of this earlier learned experience, whenever we fold a newspaper to put it in the paper rack in her presence, it triggers off a defence reflex. We could spend time desensitising her to this fear by folding a newspaper, ignoring the lips-back snarling that it produces and giving her a tit-bit; contrary to popular opinion, we would not be rewarding her for snarling, we would be changing her expectations about what a folded newspaper means. We found an easier way of overcoming the problem; we do not fold up a newspaper when she is around.

This example is the first of many where it is important that we fully understand our dogs. We do not know what has happened to the dog in the past. If a particular action triggers off an aggressive response, we should not necessarily take the view: '*No dog's gonna growl at me*'. If it is a fear response, then punishment will only increase the fear, and with it, the aggression.

Basically, a dog is a domesticated predatory pack animal. Most of them are capable of surviving in a wild state. Stray or lost dogs will quickly adjust to a nomadic existence and will soon join up with other strays to form feral packs. Luckily, in this country this is not allowed to happen to such a point that it reaches a problematical level. However, in some areas numbers of latch-key dogs do tend to form into a sort of loose feral pack; feral by day and domesticated by night.

In a feral or wild state, dogs very quickly establish a pecking order. Within this group, rank has its privileges and the instinct that drives each individual member of this group does not alter when the pack in which it lives consists of a mixture of humans and canines.

Whatever the environment the dog finds itself in, it only takes about two days to adjust and about fourteen days to recognise and exploit any area that will enable it to increase its rank. We should be very conscious of this fact when taking on a rescue dog and giving it plenty of time to settle, before we decide to lay down some house rules.

In a feral pack, the highest ranking eats first, has the choice of sleeping areas; precedes all others through narrow openings; leads the pack; defends the pack and keeps the pack together. These privileges are also granted to the highest ranking member of the domestic canine/human pack. By rights, that should be us, but all too often it turns out to be the dog.

If we inadvertently grant these privileges to the dog, then it is going to take on the responsibilities that go with the job; the result is a problem dog.

The rank restructuring advice on pp. 174–7 will show how to keep all of these areas under your control.

THE SINGLE DOG HOME

Not many people decide to take on the responsibility of a dog until they have established a stable environment in which to keep it. It may be that this will be your first experience of owning a dog, or perhaps your Mum and Dad had one when you were a child. Quite often, people take on a rescue dog to replace a previous, much loved and sadly departed pet. One of these examples will apply to you in some way and the purpose of this section is to give some advice to people who are going to introduce a dog into a household where he or she will be the only dog.

As stated above, it only takes about two days for a dog to adjust to a new environment and fourteen days to take advantage of any weakness within that environment that will enable it to increase its rank.

It usually takes humans about a month to come to terms with and learn about the peculiar habits of their new dog. By then it is too late: the dog has beaten you by a clear two weeks.

Regardless of what you believe his or her previous history has been, your new dog will have forgotten this. It will have looked at the new environment and probably thought, 'This will do for me.' Within a few days it will have 'sussed' out all of the rank-promoting areas and, over the next few days will start to establish its rights over them. We just assume that the dog is beginning to settle in.

Next, it will look at the established human rank structure and start to climb its way up it. In most cases, this is done without any member of the family recognising exactly what is happening. I have lost count of the times that I am told, 'He didn't make a sound for a couple of weeks, now we can't shut him up.' In real terms, what has happened is that the dog did not see it as his right to defend the rest of the pack initially. Over a two-week period, certain privileges were granted to him that told him that he was the highest ranking (on an instinctive level). As a result, he then took on the role that the owner had inadvertently given him. Of course he is going to bark to warn off intruders, it's his job to do so — you told him so.

Naturally, we want our dogs to bark when they hear intruders. In the wild state, dogs (or wolves) will give warning of approaching danger. Barking is designed to summon help. In a well led pack, once the higher-ranking members respond to the bark/warning, the barker should back off and allow the highest ranking animal to make the decisions. If, after you have arrived to investigate the reason why your dog has barked, you cannot stop it, you should start to think about why he or she continues to defend. As leader of your pack, it should be up to you who does or does not enter your den. As a member of your pack, your dog will help you if you initiate an attack on the intruder or if the intruder initiates an attack on you; it is not the dog's right to make that decision in your presence.

Having a single dog can often result in that dog being granted much more freedom of movement around the house than it would get if there were two or three dogs. We don't mind leaving dogs in the kitchen if there are other dogs for company, but we feel sorry about leaving a single dog on its own. If we are not careful, this can result in overattachments being formed, to the extent that it is impossible to leave the dog on its own, even if it is just to pop out and post a letter. We create what behaviourists term a separation anxiety. Anxiety-related problems of this type take various forms: house-soiling, destructiveness, howling and barking, or digging around the doors and windows in an attempt to escape and follow us. In severe cases of extreme anxiety the dog might direct its frustration on itself and self-mutilation might result, sometimes causing quite horrific injuries. This is no different from nail-biting in humans as a tension-relieving behaviour.

In my experience, this is the most common problem reported by owners who have taken on a 'rescue dog'. As I said, we tend to over-compensate for what we *think* has happened to the dog in the past. Many owners allow the new dog to sleep in their bedrooms, rather than shut it in the kitchen on its own. Most owners will not take on the responsibility of a rescue dog unless someone is at home most of the day to keep it company. The same 14-day rule applies before problems rear their ugly head. Because the dog is allowed to be with human companionship for 24 hours of every day, sleeping in the bedroom, following us from room to room, even trying to get into the loo with us, we find that if we have occasion to leave it at home on its own it cannot stand the desolation of isolation and one or more of the above problems arise. It is normal but quite wrong to return home and scold the dog for whatever it has done in our absence. This only increases the anxiety because the dog soon learns that being left alone is a prelude to being told off.

Prevention is better than cure. If you are going to take on a rescue dog that will be an only dog in your household, as with the establishment of the rank structure, start as you mean to go on. By all means make the dog feel wanted, but also make sure that doors can be shut on it as you move around the house. Right from day one, teach him that being left in the kitchen for ten minutes on his own will actually bring the reward of you returning and giving him a tit-bit. This is not really any different from saying to our children, 'I'm just popping down to the shops, if you're good I'll bring you something back.'

THE MULTI-DOG HOME

Dogs are far superior to humans when it comes to establishing clear-cut rules and regulations; if we allow them to do so. This is the whole point of this section. Unless you have selected a dog of similar breed, age, size, sex and dominance level as the resident dog, then, left to their own devices, dogs will very quickly settle down and live together in perfect harmony.

The first consideration before choosing a rescue dog is that it is usually better to choose the complete opposite in all respects to the dog or dogs that you already have. It is always better to conduct the initial introduction 'off-territory' and preferably on completely neutral ground, so that neither dog has the advantage of territorial rights. After observing their behaviour together on loose leads and being satisfied that it is fairly passive, let them run together and let dogs be dogs. There may be some fairly dominant postures from one dog towards the other, but this is perfectly normal if one dog takes a liberty that the other doesn't think it has the right to take. They will sort it out providing we do not interfere. The danger is that we might rush in and upset the balance, either by putting off the inevitable normal procedure of them sorting out dominance/submissive levels, or scolding one dog because we think it started the trouble and subsequently raising the status of the other. Normally, this sort of rank structure confrontation — although frightening in some cases to watch and listen to — results in no damage being caused to either dog. The importance of the initial (on leash) introduction being fairly passive must be stressed.

If damage is caused to either dog during this or later confrontations, the question should be asked: are these two dogs temperamentally compatible? If you suspect the answer is no, seek advice from the rescue centre before the final decision is made about keeping the newcomer. Your decision to give a home to a rescue dog should not result in the quality of life for you and the dogs being affected; constant aggressive confrontations are obviously distressing to both species and it is easier to make a sensible decision sooner rather than later.

Provided this initial introduction has been conducted properly and you are reasonably confident that the dogs are compatible, when you get them home, continue the 'let dogs be dogs' theme. The biggest problem tends to be that owners usually regard the dog that has been there the longest as the one that should be the highest ranking. Without thinking, we grant top dog privileges to this dog and this can lead to problems. Humans may have a system of seniority status, but dogs don't. Once residency becomes established they need to establish the pecking order, and the fact that one of these dogs might have a few years' service longer than the other carries no weight at all. You should recognise this fact and accept it. Favouring the wrong dog will cause trouble.

Most good rescue centres have a back-up advice service, and the new owner should take full advantage of it if he or she is in any doubt about what to do under certain circumstances. Some well-timed and sensible advice can result in the new dog settling into your environment without any trouble. Failure to seek advice can result in the dog being returned to the shelter and possibly facing euthanasia because it appears impossible to re-home.

S

Sensitivity

In the past, when it came to training dogs, advice was generally given on how it should be done, regardless of the breed. The instructor would stand in the middle of the hall shouting the same training instructions to a group of people who were handling a wide variety of dogs. Miniature Poodle, Dobermann, Rottweiler and Sheltie owners were instructed: *'About turn, dog's name, command "heel", check your dogs, praise your dogs, etc. etc.'*

The big, bold Rotties and Dobermanns would probably be able to take all this shouting, feet-clumping and neck-jerking in their stride, but the Miniature Poodles and the Shelties would find it all too much for their more sensitive natures.

Sensitivity can be divided into various categories: touch, sound, sight and mental. Owners should be aware of their own dog's particular sensitivity (or insensitivity) in all these areas before attempting to teach their dog anything. For example, the Collie, because of the job of work it has been bred to do, is obviously a very sight-sensitive dog, capable of picking up and reacting to the slightest movement. It is also highly trainable because in general the breed is extremely mentally sensitive, tending to be 'in tune' with their owners' emotions, often giving the impression that they are so clever that they can anticipate what the owner is thinking. This mental sensitivity, however, can have the reverse effect with the short-tempered, hard-handed handler, who can quickly destroy the character of this workaholic type of dog.

Dogs that have been specifically bred for crashing through gorse and bracken for hour after hour in search of game are generally touch-insensitive, as are many of the terrier breeds which have been bred to stand four square against an often well-armed adversary. But although certain breeds are more likely to be more or less sensitive in a particular area than another breed, each and every dog is individual.

Taking the view, therefore, that all dogs should be trained with choke chains is really an admission by advocates of this method that they are unaware of the variations in touch-sensitivity between breeds and certain individuals within those breeds. Telling an owner that his extremely sound-sensitive Sheltie — which is quivering in a corner because the Rottie owner's hob-nailed boots, crashing on the wooden floor of the dog club, are frightening the life out of it — will get used to it, is an admission that they are not aware of sound-sensitivity. Not recognising the fact that an owner's frustration or embarrassment at performing in front of other people might be affecting the ability to learn of his mentally-sensitive dog; not being able to advise an owner that the reason why his dog is anticipating a command is because it is very sight-sensitive, and inadvertently he is telegraphing his next command by adopting a certain posture prior to giving that command — these also are admissions about the trainer's lack of awareness in these areas.

For us to be able to train our dogs, or for people to be able to teach others to train their dogs, these sensitivities should be assessed and the training techniques engineered to take them into account. The following case is similar to the leash-phobic dog described on p. 157, but the reasons are entirely different.

Question
Why does my dog run and hide whenever I pick up his lead and chain to take him for a walk? He does enjoy his walks once he is outside, in fact I have a job to catch him again to bring him home. All my other dogs have gone potty in the past when I have picked up their leads, so I don't understand why this one acts so differently. Any ideas, please?

Answer
Almost certainly your dog — like me — does not like the chain. You may have noticed that when you do catch him and attempt to slip the chain on, he turns his head from side to side. I fully accept the fact that the choke chain has become the standard piece of equipment for exercising and training dogs, but when a situation arises where a dog, who likes his walks, will not be caught to be taken on one, then it is time to ask some serious questions.

Surprisingly, your question is not unusual. Many people have experienced the same problem and have lived with it for years. They take the view that because the dog is contained within the house, it is not really a problem because it always hides in the same place. At the end of the walk, the dog does not actually run away — it just does not come close enough to catch and the only problem is being able to devise some new trick to tempt it close enough to grab it. In almost every case, the two common denominators have been a choke chain and a touch-sensitive dog.

It is relatively easy to discover whether this is the problem in your case. First of all, you need to know the level of your dog's touch-sensitivity. With your dog facing you in the sit position, gently lift a front paw and with your finger and thumb take hold of the webbed skin between the toes. Counting from one to ten, gradually increase the pressure (the object of the exercise is to test your dog's reactivity, not to inflict pain). The vast majority of dogs will give a little whimper and make a token effort to pull their paw away at about count seven or eight. If your dog objects earlier, this will show the level of touch-sensitivity peculiar to your dog.

If you get a reading of three or four, I would advise you very strongly to 'chuck the choke'. An ordinary leather buckle collar will suit your dog and, if it is worn all the time, he will respond happily and readily whenever you pick up his lead to take him out. It might take a few days for him to get over his learned aversion to what he 'thinks' is a painful experience, but patience will bring reward. Think of things from his point of view. He really enjoys his walks, but going on them hurts!

Socialise
It is important when choosing a new puppy to take a careful look at the temperament of both the mother and the father, because this will have a direct genetic bearing on the future temperament of your dog when he or she becomes an adult. This careful selection will be wasted, however, if the puppy is not socialised at an early age.

All animals, humans included, go through critical periods of development, and where pet dogs are concerned, probably the most important is the period from seven to around eighteen to twenty weeks. It is during this period that they should learn what life is all about in a domestic and practical environment (the environment in which they will live their lives). Early exposure to all sorts of stimuli — children, traffic, other dogs, strangers, vets — but always under rewarding circumstances, will teach a youngster to be confident in similar circumstances when he gets older. Later than twenty weeks, and the young dog is entering a different period of development; it is now much more difficult to build up his confidence in unfamiliar environments.

Unfortunately, the practice of isolating our dogs until their vaccination programme is complete means that, for many dogs, they do not experience life outside the security of our homes until late into this socialisation period. Many dogs miss out on it altogether, and these are the dogs which generally pose problems later in life. Of course it is important that we protect our puppies against the killer canine diseases — parvo virus, distemper, hardpad, hepatitis, leptospirosis — but we should also consider balancing the risk of exposing them to infection against not allowing them to develop behaviourally. The Guide Dogs for the Blind Association have conducted extensive research for many years into the effects of early socialisation, and their results speak for themselves. Guide dog puppies are *carried* into the big wide world to meet and greet people at six weeks of age. Naturally, the puppy walkers do not allow their charges to run around loose in a public park, nor do they take them to areas where the risk of canine infection is high, but they do expose them to as many different stimuli as possible — as early as possible.

Question
I am planning on getting a puppy shortly and I don't want him to grow up like my last dog which was very aggressive towards people and other dogs. I have read that it is best to get them out and about as soon as possible and that I should start training him as soon as I can.

Unfortunately, my local dog club will not accept dogs into their classes until they are at least six months old. Surely, this is far too old for them to start socialising with other dogs?

Answer
A lot of dog clubs still operate this six-months age rule, although when I ask them why, they don't really know. Some say that the Kennel Club insists on it, some say that you don't

really know what problems you have with your dog until that age; some even say that a dog is not capable of learning until that age. In fact, puppies are transmitting adult brain waves at between seven and eight weeks — they may not have the stamina or the ability to concentrate for long periods, but they do have the ability to learn. If we don't start to teach them the things that we want them to learn, they are going to teach themselves (through self-reward) all the things that we don't want them to learn. Come the age of six months, we are then faced with the task of corrective training because we have allowed habits to develop and have missed out on the dog's most influential learning period. In short, there is no substitute for good early experience.

There is an increasing number of more enlightened trainers who recognise the worth of early learning and are running puppy kindergarten classes. These are for puppies between the ages of 12 to 18 weeks — 12 weeks because this is the earliest that their vaccination programme can be completed (bear in mind that they can still be carefully socialised before then) and 18 weeks because after this age they enter a different stage of development. In these classes, big breed puppies learn how to behave with little breed puppies, and little puppies learn not to be frightened of big puppies. Mums, dads and children of all ages are encouraged to attend, and while the children are running around, generally behaving like children, the adults are handling all the puppies to get them used to strangers. Basic exercises like the sit, down, stay, come and heel are taught, using positive reinforcement as a training aid. The children are also encouraged to teach these exercises to their puppies.

The effectiveness of these puppy classes has been researched and proven in America by Dr Ian Dunbar (Hon. Veterinary adviser to the APBC). He has shown beyond doubt that early training and socialisation result in a confident, well-adjusted adult dog, and these dogs rarely show aggression towards people or other dogs. I would suggest that you talk to your veterinary surgeon to find out where the nearest puppy kindergarten is to your area. (*See also* Puppies, p. 171.)

Spaying

From a long-term health point of view, if you have no intention of breeding from your bitch, most veterinary surgeons would advise you to have her spayed. An entire female is more likely to develop infections of the womb and tumours as she gets older, than a spayed female is. There is very little evidence, however, to support the theory that spaying is useful from a behavioural point of view, unless we are dealing with a case of (in house) female-to-female aggression which occurs only around the time of a season. The chemical signals (pheromones) given off by a bitch coming into season can directly influence the hormonal status of other bitches around it. This becomes evident when you consider that a multi-bitch household will eventually establish a pattern of all coming into season at around the same time. As mentioned in Chapter 5 under M. Mounting, only high-ranking wolves come into season, probably because their pheromones suppress the reproductive cycle of lower ranking females. Except in a few rare cases, the opposite seems to be true of the domesticated version (the dog) and this can sometimes cause problems. Two females in season within the same household would suggest that they are both of equal rank and competitive fighting can break out with seemingly the least provocation. Unlike male dominance struggles which are usually over once one male submits or flees, females will sometimes fight to the death. Having the lower ranked female spayed can often overcome this problem.

Except for these circumstances, having a bitch spayed to help with a behavioural problem seems to have little effect — indeed my APBC colleague, Dr Valerie O'Farrell, conducted some research into the effects of spaying on the behaviour of bitches and concluded that there were no improvements to be gained. Interestingly, she found evidence to show that in 40 per cent of cases where bitches under two years of age were showing dominant aggression, they became worse after spaying.

As with castrating males, my personal opinion is — if you don't want to breed from your dog, it is kinder to have her neutered, but bearing in mind Dr O'Farrell's findings, dominant aggression in the female should be overcome before you do so.

Question
I have a three-year-old Japanese Shiba Inu called Acer (pretty Japanese small tree) and just recently she has started to act most strangely. She has always been a very loving dog, and still is most of the time. However, just lately, she has started to become very grumpy when she is in her bed; occasionally she growls when we go near her food bowl; she digs holes in the

garden and puts my husband's plastic flower pots in them; if she gets hold of a newspaper, she shreds it to pieces; and she scratches the carpets behind one of the chairs in the lounge or in the corner of the dining-room.

Answer

Without doubt, Acer is having a phantom pregnancy: she thinks that the plant pots are her babies — funny, but sad for her. Although this foxy-looking breed is still quite rare in this country, they are in fact one of the spitz breeds and, as such, fairly primitive in their instincts. I would guarantee that Acer was in season recently and, assuming she is not pregnant, the hormonal changes that she has undergone are telling her that she is — or has been. No doubt if you looked, you would find that she is also producing milk to feed her plant pots.

If she is guarding her bed and her food against you, this would indicate a fairly dominant attitude, although perfectly natural for a mother who has a high regard for her rank within the environment.

Her digging in the garden is a nesting behaviour, as is her scratching at the carpets and shredding paper. She now regards the plant pots as her puppies, whereas some dogs focus their attentions on a slipper or one of their toys. Quite often the advice would be to let her get on with it and the problem will eventually disappear. This of course is perfectly true, but I find it sad that these very maternal bitches are allowed to endure this stressful period without help. Quite often, some hormonal treatment from your vet will alleviate the problem; alternatively, there are homoeopathic remedies available, which are ideally suited to this sort of problem, and your vet will refer you to a qualified person if you wish to take this course. This sort of behaviour is not uncommon in highly maternal bitches and, in human terms, resembles the psychological state of the woman who steals babies. With humans, we recognise their need for help, and in my opinion we should do the same for dogs.

Provided you can overcome the dominant aspect of her character, if you want to breed from her in the future she will probably be a wonderful mother. If you don't want to breed from her, then for her own psychological good I would suggest you have her spayed; but again I would stress the importance of reducing her dominant attitude (*see* Rank reversal, p. 174).

Stealing
See Play/possession (question), p. 166.

Stress
Although much recognised in humans, stress is rarely considered as a contributory factor in behavioural changes in dogs. In humans, doctors recognise the fact that stress is a major cause of many physical and psychological illnesses, yet we are less ready to consider how our dogs cope with the stresses and strains that our modern environment places upon them.

We might recognise as fearfulness the fact that some dogs, on being taken into a dog club for the first time (for example), will salivate, hold their ears back, tuck their tails between their legs, leave sweaty paw prints on the floor and, in some cases, urinate. Unfortunately, all too often the advice given to the owner is that they will 'get used to it'. What we don't recognise is that prolonged exposure to this fearful environment will drain the dog's stress reserve level and its ability to cope — much as it does in people.

At the time of writing, we are three weeks into the Gulf War and I have been listening to a human psychologist talking about soldiers who suffer from battle stress. His theory was that this type of stress should be treated in the battle zone, because removing the soldier from the fearful environment would give the body such reward that the resultant coping behaviour would be to run away if that soldier were exposed to the same fearful stimuli. This I can understand in theory, but unless the other side is asked to shoot a little more quietly, I don't know how the stress can be treated *in situ*. We do not have to continue to expose our dogs to fearful situations; we can remove them and consider other ways of achieving our aims. If the dog is stressed by a club environment, it is unable to learn. By employing a good private trainer, we overcome the stress factor and are able to teach the dog what we want it to learn.

This type of reaction is called negative stress and is not only evident in dog clubs (I hasten to add that most dogs cope quite well with a club environment), it can also be seen in a vet's waiting-room, usually taking the form of excessive hair loss and, in the case of my Japanese Akita, trembling and escape behaviour whenever the door is opened. Fortunately, our dogs are not exposed to this type of environment long enough or often enough for it to cause long-term physical or behavioural side-effects. However, stressful domestic environments can and do affect the behaviour of a lot of dogs because they are exposed to it on a daily basis. Marriage upheaval, regular drunken arguments, stroppy teenage children, are often major causative factors in behavioural problems in dogs.

This is one of the reasons why I and my colleagues in the APBC prefer to discuss the dog's problem with the whole family. Not that this information is volunteered, but certain clues point us in the right direction and we are able tactfully to direct the conversation to confirm our suspicions. Quite often this will result in a second, more private consultation with the worried owner to explain that the cure for his dog's behaviour lies in the family's hands.

The coping behaviour of dogs suffering from stress will take a variety of forms. Negative stress has already been described, and I imagine that many pet owners will have noticed how their dogs 'head for the hills' when an argument erupts at home. This is normal for most dogs and does not necessarily create problems — only prolonged exposure will do this. Some people report that their dogs become very boisterous during arguments, as though they were trying to referee it. This is what I term a positive reaction and again will only create problems if overdosed. This kind of behaviour is often misinterpreted as disobedience, especially in a dog club environment. The dog that appears to be handling things quite well will suddenly start to act like a hyperactive puppy, especially under circumstances where the owner is trying to get the dog to do something which it does not seem to understand — the owner's temper starts to show and the dog starts to act like a loony. It is very similar to the human reaction of trying to defuse a situation through joking and reverting to childish behaviour. This type of coping behaviour will eventually lead to positive stress unless the cause is removed.

Some introverted dogs will centre their stress-coping behaviour upon themselves, and it is not unusual to hear of dogs that appear to self-mutilate under certain conditions. Scratching, paw-licking or nibbling are often classic symptoms, but flank-sucking might also be evident. It should be understood that these behaviours might be indicative of some medical problem, and it is only when the dog behaves in this way under certain circumstances that a stress reaction should be suspected and the root cause looked for.

Like people, I think that the vast majority of dogs are exposed to stressful situations on a fairly regular basis. Also like people, some dogs can cope easily and some cannot. Working as I do from two distinctly different environments — one a very relaxed, almost domestic environment in my consulting rooms at my Surrey practice; the other a veterinary consulting room in London — I see a noticeable difference in the way that dogs behave depending upon their surroundings.

In the less formal environment, it is the owners who are generally more on edge at the start of the consultation and, as described in Chapter 4, dominant-type dogs tend to act in what is often described as a hyperactive manner. If I offer food, it is generally snatched from my hand in a very yobbish, 'gimme that' manner. I suspect that this is caused by the dog's recognition that the pack feels insecure, therefore a leader has to come to the fore. If the dog sees its role as that of leader, but is not genetically equipped for that role (in a wolf pack or feral dog pack it would not be the Alpha figure), this can lead to what I term leadership stress. This type of dog has not suddenly gained that view of its role within the canine/human pack, it had that idea before it arrived. Much like people who are burdened with ultimate responsibility, this might have a disastrous effect on its health — it certainly does on its behaviour. (I would add that this theory has not been proven and I hope to do some research into it in the future. My comments under Epilepsy (p. 113) would seem to confirm my suspicions.)

On the other hand, dogs that I see at the Woodthorpe Veterinary Group in London act in an entirely different manner. In this environment, it is the dogs and not the owners that are more insecure. They exhibit increased hair loss, they are subdued and very unassuming. If offered food, they generally refuse to take it. Both types of behaviour are stress reactions and should be recognised as such, but as previously stated, it is not how the dog copes that is the problem, it is whether the dog has to cope over a prolonged and regular period.

Submissiveness
This behaviour is described in Chapter 5 under U. Urination. The following case history describes how to overcome the problem in an adult dog.

Much like the case described under Games (p. 126), this case involved a two-year-old male Golden Retriever and the reported problem was that it urinated when the owners came home. It took just a few minutes to establish the fact that it was classic submissive urination. It took some time to convince his very dominant owners that it was an involuntary and perfectly normal canine reaction to the presence of a more dominant animal; they were convinced that the dog was doing it on purpose to punish them for leaving him at home. As you can imagine, their response was to tell the dog off each time, which further convinced the dog that it should show submission. Contrary to how it might seem, the owners were very caring people who loved their dog dearly; they just could not understand why it behaved in this way and continued to do so even though (in their words) *'He knows he's doing wrong'*. Once we had cleared up the misunderstanding between the two species (human and canine), the following programme was advised which quickly overcame the problem.

The owners were told to open the door, but instead of approaching the dog, they should walk into the garden calling for their dog to join them. This meant that they were not presenting a full-frontal dominant posture to the dog, but a more submissive rear view; it also meant that any urination would take place in the garden, not the house — less mess, less tension. They were also advised that rather than stroking the dog to greet him, they should tell him to sit for a tit-bit reward. This would give him something else to think about and, as the 'sit for food' reward is something that the majority of dogs learn very early, a behaviour that the dog was confident in performing. All this was designed to overcome the established greeting procedure and to teach the dog some fresh expectations about what the return of his owners was all about.

We now needed a programme to build the dog's general confidence, and this was achieved by reversing some of the principles laid out under Rank reversal (p. 174). Particular emphasis was placed on playing competitive games with him, especially tug-of-war which the dog should win. It was stressed that, initially, their dog would not want to play, basically because he would be convinced that he could never win and would therefore not even dream of competing. They were told to persevere and, at the first attempt he made to take the rag or toy, the owners should allow him to win.

It took a few days before they reported that their dog was readily playing with a tug toy, and they stated that there was a marked change in his general attitude. How they described it was that he appeared to walk around the house with a bit of a swagger. It was encouraging to hear also that there was a marked reduction in his piddling activities. They were naturally pleased with the progress that they had made so far, but it was especially nice for me to hear that their greatest reward came from understanding their dog a little better.

Having advised them not to let the swagger get too pronounced, it was left that they would contact me if there were any future problems. During a one-to-one two-hour consultation, I get to know my clients quite well and many have become good friends. It may therefore seem strange if I say that I am pleased that I have not heard from them again.

T

Telephones and Television

It is quite common for people to complain that whenever they are on the phone their dog either asks to go out, barks all the time or wants to play, usually with something that they should not have, like a shoe or an item of clothing. Some dogs get quite aggressive towards their owners whenever the phone rings. To a lesser extent, but certainly not an uncommon problem, is the complaint that the dog becomes disruptive during certain television programmes — most noticeably the very popular soap called *Neighbours*. In almost every case the problem is attention-seeking, and if we look at things from the dog's point of view, we can see how easily they learn to do it.

Probably the first training exercise we embark upon with our new puppy is toilet training. The object is to get the pup to go to the door leading to the garden and bark to be let out (or some other signal). The first time this happens, humans appear from all over the place — out of the loo, out of the bath, from talking on the phone, from watching the television. Praise is heaped upon the puppy and it is allowed to go out. As far as we are concerned, the object of the exercise has been reached, but do we always appreciate what the puppy might have learnt?

Take the telephone, for example, and let's consider what this means to the puppy. Usually, whenever a human enters the room he or she pays attention to the puppy, either by stroking it or just speaking to it; the only time this does not happen is when that damn bell rings. On these occasions, humans rush into the room, totally ignore the pup and speak to some stupid bit of plastic. The puppy can have no idea that there is another person on the other end of the phone, so that this strange behaviour is perplexing. It is an interesting fact that whenever a dog becomes confused, it will usually perform the first exercise it was taught and in which it is confident that it is doing the right thing — usually the sit.

In general, this goes unnoticed by the person on the phone, so that puppy performs some other behaviour which has proved rewarding in the past: it goes to the door and whines. BINGO! Instant reward! The human says to the piece of plastic. *'Hang on a moment, the puppy is asking to go to the loo,'* puts the phone down and praises the pup. We now have the start of a learned behaviour pattern, an action is rewarded and so the chances are increased of it being repeated. During my talks to pet groups and clubs up and down the country I often ask how many people have dogs that behave in this or similar fashion when they are on the phone. My conclusion from their answers is that over 50 per cent of dogs' bladders in this country are directly connected to the telephone system.

Alternatively, the dog might pick up one of its toys, and although the person on the phone might notice this, they don't pay any attention to it. If, however, the puppy picks up something forbidden, it is rewarded by getting the attention of the owner. These behaviours are not performed through logical thought processes, they are simply reactions to the confusion of the human's strange response to the ringing bell, a form of displacement activity that gets rewarded.

Although it sounds like a joke, I and some of my other APBC colleagues have been asked why some dogs become disruptive whilst *Neighbours* is on the television (or some other popular programme). Resisting the urge to make some scathing comment about the quality of some TV programmes, it usually proves to be the case that this is a programme that the whole family sits down to watch. Generally, Dad might watch a sports programme or the news; Mum might like to watch a quiz programme; whilst the kids tune in to a pop programme. Most of the time, there is always someone who is not staring at the screen and can give the dog the attention that it demands. When they all sit down, the dog's attention-seeking behaviour does not get any worse than usual, it just becomes obvious.

Question
How do I stop my dog barking when I am on the phone? I live alone and my dog is my constant companion, so I suppose he gets jealous when I speak to someone else. I must admit that I haven't been too cross with him for barking because, as you can

imagine, I don't want to curb his guarding abilities, but he seems to be getting worse. If I shut him out he just scratches the door and barks even louder.

Answer
Telling him off will not negate his usefulness as a guard dog, neither will it help to overcome your problem. No doubt, because you live alone with your dog, any normal guarding behaviour is rewarded. However, rewarding his behaviour when you are on the phone will encourage him — as will telling him off. In both scenarios you are giving the dog the attention that he is demanding and, like children, dogs don't care whether that attention is good or bad. The answer is to take away the reward that he gets from behaving in this unacceptable manner. You should first of all understand that he is not jealous — he cannot see, or does not know who is on the other end of the phone. All he does know is that you are not paying attention to him (something that I suspect he understandably gets too much of until the phone rings).

What we need to do is take away the reward (attention, good or bad) and sound aversion therapy is ideal for this kind of problem. Whilst speaking on the phone, we create a sound that has already been introduced to the dog in such a way that he has learnt that a particular action creates an unpleasant reaction — even if the only conversation that is going on is an explanation about the funny noise. The object of the exercise is simply to ignore the dog, but to make attention-seeking unpleasant (*see* Appendix, Sound Aversion Therapy, for details). Rewarding the dog at the end of the conversation is not a good idea at the start of the behaviour modification programme. There is a danger that he might start to anticipate the reward and this will increase the excitement. The dog should learn that whilst you are on the phone, he should remain quiet.

If you contact your local telephone engineers and tell them what the problem is, they will tell you what number to dial to get your phone to ring so that you can organise some dummy training sessions. Alternatively, get someone to call you at a specified time, simply to have a 'rhubarb, rhubarb' conversation. In this way a concerted effort can be made to take away the reward without having to explain your weird behaviour to someone who has called you unexpectedly.

Territorial

Chapter 5 explains the basic instincts that govern the territorial behaviour of most dogs; this applies to both big dogs and little dogs, regardless of breed. In fact, many of the behavioural problems described in this book so far relate to territorial behaviour. We need to understand a basic fact of life: we may arrange a mortgage on our property that covers so many square metres, but our dog is going to take every opportunity to increase our freehold. Some dogs are happy to regard their beds as their territory; some the house; some the house and garden; some the road outside their house; some the park where they are regularly exercised. At the end of the day, the problem faced by most pet owners is whether the dog regards it as his or her duty to defend territory, or the duty of the owner. It is this self-regard for responsibility that is the key to territorial aggression, or other related problems (*see* 'Rank reversal' p. 174).

With fiercely territorial dogs, it often helps to broaden their horizons a little more. If, for example, the dog regards the garden as his or her personal space, increased off-territory exercise, a decrease in the time spent in the garden and the removal of some of his favourite possessions (like his football, tug toy, frisbee) which almost certainly he will keep in this area, can help to reduce this territorial attitude. This distribution of possessions is a form of territory marking, not through the chemical signals achieved by urinating at specific points around the boundary, but by visual displays of property and belongings.

This is really no different from the way we behave when we occupy a hotel room; it is not until we have scattered our belongings around the room that we regard it as ours. It is as well to remember also that some breeds have a greater disposition towards territorial aggression than others — the guarding breeds, for example — and when they are puppies, we should be careful not to encourage what will be a natural instinct anyway.

Observing territorial behaviour within a mixed breed multi-dog environment is a fascinating exercise. Within my own pack of four dogs there is a clear-cut rank structure. The Weimaraner (Oliver) is the unquestionable leader, followed by the Japanese Akita (Yoko), the Collie (Inch) and then the Jack Russell (Chip). If one of them barks at a passer-by, they all join in until Oliver arrives on the scene and then the rest shut up. In terms of guarding territory, my wife and I only have to control

Oliver; he controls the rest. There is no aggression between them, just an understanding of where they rank within the pack structure. However, indoors we have the curious situation whereby Oliver is granted top dog status by the other dogs throughout the house except in one room, and this is controlled by the lowest ranking dog, Chip, the Jack Russell — in this room she thinks she is a Jack Rottweiler. Chip belongs to my step-daughter Joanne, given to her when she was nine years old (she is now sixteen). Chip has been Jo's constant companion and, contrary to what I advise my clients with dominant dogs, sleeps in Jo's bedroom. On very cold nights she will worm her way into the bed and has been known to snap at Jo's feet if she moves them in the night — yes, you've got it; Chip is a typical 'Toad Russell'. She definitely suffers from what I call 'little dog syndrome', because she is granted privileges that bigger dogs would never get. She is constantly being picked up and cuddled, she occupies any handy knee she can find; where my bigger dogs are fenced in, Chip can escape through the smallest hole (we live on a common so do not have the problem of traffic).

On top of all this, she has her own territory within the den, and woe betide the higher ranking dogs that try to invade it. For some curious reason, like the human pack members, the rest of the dogs seem to tolerate this and do in fact respect her aggressive 'stay out of my space' attitude. Away from this room, the other dogs just need to look at her when she 'gets out of her pram' and she will instantly display submissive body postures. This strange reversal of rank, where the lowest ranking dog can achieve top dog status within the territory of a higher ranking dog, has arisen through human interference and does not seem to cause any problems. The reason that I have included this tale about my own dogs is to show that this situation can arise within any domestic environment without people realising just how territorial dogs can be, and might well lead to problems in the pack. It also goes to show that my dogs are not exactly paragons of virtue, despite the fact that I counsel other owners on their dogs' problems; my excuse is that I could cure them, but I would have nothing left to study if they were perfect and I intend to stick to that excuse.

Question

Why does my three-year-old Cairn Terrier dog always try to
bite people's ankles when they go to leave the house? He is very
friendly to them when they arrive and all the time they are
there, but he gets awfully aggressive when they go towards the
door. The only other place where he is aggressive to visitors is
at the gate. If we pick him up as our visitors leave, or try to put
him in another room, he can sometimes become aggressive
towards us. The rest of the time he is the sweetest of dogs and
really no trouble at all.

Answer

I think the answer to your problem is quite simply that he is
defending his territory. We would normally assume that this
would be the house, but if you look at his behaviour — aggressive at the gate and at the door when people leave (not when they
arrive) – then we can see that, in both cases, they are entering
the garden and I can guarantee that this is where your dog
keeps his favourite possessions or bones and probably enjoys
spending a great deal of time. It would seem to me that he views
his role within your pack as defender of the garden, whilst it is
your responsibility to defend the home.

Have a good look round the garden to see how many treasures he is hoarding out there and, in particular, where he keeps
them. I bet his favourite articles are kept near the gate and the
back door. Collect them all up when he is not looking and place
them in a pile away from these key areas, then watch as he
industriously redistributes them back to the original places. If
this is the case, then clearly this is the root cause of your problem with visitors.

You will need to take possession of these articles yourself;
they are no longer his, they are yours, and you will let him have
the occasional one to borrow when it suits you. You will also
have to make sure that he spends less time in the garden and
more time on off-territory walks (it is very easy to let the dog
exercise himself when there is a big garden in which to do it).
Indoors, you will need to attach a light trailing line to his collar,
so that you can take control of him just before your visitors prepare to leave. As they do, they can produce one of the possessions that you now own, tell him to sit, reward him with the
toy and then leave. Five minutes later, repossess the toy yourself and put it away until your next visitor. It is usually a good

idea to arrange for friends and neighbours to drop in to see you at specific times, simply to teach your dog that visitors leaving is a prelude to reward. (See reference to John Rogerson, p. 96.)

Training

See Instructors, p. 146, and Obedience classes, p. 161.

U

Unusual Cases

From time to time, I and my colleagues in the APBC come across the odd case that is quite bizarre. Dominance aggression that has been encouraged by the female owner breast-feeding the dog. (*Yes, you did read that properly, it really was happening — and it was an adult male dog!*) Dogs that have a hatred of light bulbs and as soon as anyone walks under one, will use the person's back as a springboard and smash the bulb on their heads. Dogs that howl at the new moon, even if it is obscured by cloud. But I think the most unusual case that I have had to deal with was the dog that was frightened of bones.

Frisky was a two-year-old male Bull Terrier cross. He was originally called B'stard after the character in the television programme *The New Statesman*, but his owners found it too embarrassing to shout his name in the local park, so it had to be changed. My initial reaction when they told me about Frisky's fear was, don't give him any bones, but the problem went deeper than that. Every day his owners, Peter Bessant and his girlfriend Claire, took Frisky to Peter's mother while they went off to work. On the way they had to pass an abattoir and this sent Frisky into total panic to the point where he became aggressive if they tried to force him past. Because they did not own a car, it meant that Peter's mother had to drive to their house to collect Frisky and then drive him back to her house.

His fear of bones, however, was not linked to the abattoir and the possible smell of death. Who knows what dogs can sense! It had become evident earlier, before they moved into the area, but had never posed a problem. As with my initial reaction, they just did not give him bones. Prior to their arrival, I had placed a fresh marrow-bone in the paddock outside my office (I really wanted to see the dog's reaction for myself). I was warned that as soon as he got even the smell of it, he would panic and might well become very aggressive. I must admit, I expected to see symptoms of food-orientated aggression.

How wrong I proved to be! Having taken all the details that I needed about his daily routine and behaviour under certain circumstances — all of which seemed perfectly normal — we put him on an extending lead and took him out to the paddock. As soon as Frisky caught the scent of the bone, his whole body posture became rigid, the pupils of his eyes dilated, his hackles rose, and for about ten seconds he remained motionless. Then he erupted into what I can only describe as a blind panic. He ran to the full extent of the lead in an attempt to get away. When this proved impossible he thrashed about, still trying to escape. Then it was almost as if he realised that the reason he couldn't get away was because I was holding on to the other end of the lead, at which point he started to run towards me. Now a Bull Terrier cross looks cute, but a cross Bull Terrier is an entirely different kettle of fish. Using all my knowledge and experience of canine behaviour, I took the necessary steps to defuse this potentially aggressive confrontation. Roughly translated, that means I panicked and let go of the lead. Frisky ran for my open office door, extending lead bouncing along behind him and no doubt adding to his fear. We found him wedged between my filing cabinet and the wall, shaking like a leaf.

All my family are great believers in homoeopathic remedies and in particular the Bach remedies (*see* p. 80). Because we use them ourselves, I was able to give Frisky a few drops of something called Rescue Remedy to help him overcome his terror and panic. This might sound like throwing two bat's wings and a dragon's claw into a cauldron, but they really do work in many cases. These are usually prescribed with the referring vet's permission and through my colleague Mr Richard Bleckman (Hon Vet adviser to the APBC) at the Woodthorpe Veterinary Group. In this case, needs must, and as there can be no harmful side-effects, a first aid remedy was called for. Both Peter and Claire were amazed at how quickly Frisky recovered, but even though the bone had been removed, we still had trouble getting him out of the door at the end of the session.

Normally, for phobias of this sort, I would recommend a phobic desensitisation programme (*see* Desensitise, p. 105). In this case, the reaction was so pronounced, the panic so potentially dangerous, not only to the person holding the lead but also to the health of the dog, that I decided that behaviour therapy was not really the answer. The problem could be avoided, albeit at the expense and effort of Peter's mother. I suggested that they might like to discuss with their vet the possibility of being referred to a homoeopathic vet so that the phobia could be treated more specifically. I later heard that this was the course of action they decided to take, with great but not total improvement. Peter and Claire came up with the final solution: they moved house, bought a car and made sure that Frisky would never get near another bone.

Considering the fact that many of my clients start their conversation with the phrase: 'You are our last hope', and mindful of the fact that many successes are achieved through the relatively new science of behaviour therapy, it takes the Peters and Claires of this world and their dogs (probably aptly named B'stard in the first place) to show us that sometimes, through studying behaviour we may be able to understand the mind of the dog, but we shall never fully understand how the dog's mind works.

V

Looking through the alphabet so far, I see that I have covered the vast majority of pet owners' behaviour problems, including the W, X, Y and Z sections. For example, Walking would be included under Heelwork or Pulling. For X, Y and Z, if you have problems that start with these letters, I would need to see you privately, because I cannot think of any behaviour that could be so listed. Therefore 'V' becomes the final alphabetical section — rightly so, because the only relevant heading that I can think of is:

Veterinary surgeon
The new science of behaviour therapy is gaining momentum all the time in this country. Although ideas are slowly changing, many 'died-in-the-wool' trainers will continue to blame owners for the fact that their dogs have not been trained properly and declare that the fault lies with them. As I have stated many times in this book: for sure, training is important, but what is more important is understanding the animal you live with. Some vets also take the view that strict discipline is the key to success and will still recommend the rolled-up newspaper technique to enforce the word NO, or the 'rub the nose in the mess they have made' technique to teach house-training (few, admittedly, but enough who are still active and adamant). Thankfully, more and more vets are appreciating the fact that behaviour counsellors can give time to their clients to discuss the problems that they are faced with, offer a punishment-free programme to overcome the problem, and liaise with them about the ongoing programme. Without doubt, many vets in this country are quite capable of advising programmes of behaviour modification to their clients, but with a waiting-room full of people with sick pets they just do not have the time to do so.

The purpose of this section, therefore, is to thank the vets who are more enlightened, to accept the fact that they are our bread and butter, to hope that the treatment we advise is well received by their clients and that the results justify their referral, and to hope that in the future behaviour therapy will become just as important to veterinary medicine as it has to human medicine.

Just after writing this section, I received the following letter from one of my past clients. With her permission, I have included some brief extracts from it, because it confirms the results obtained from the application of some of the aforementioned techniques.

Randolph, my Cairn Terrier, and I came to see you at your Surrey practice in December and again at Woodthorpe in February. You may recall calling him a real 'one off' during our first visit and you changed his diet. Within a week or two we noticed a difference: 1. He would calm down for brief periods. 2. His front leg stopped shaking. 3. He stopped scratching his bottom on the floor (worms and anal gland problems had been previously ruled out if you remember).

After our next visit to you at the Woodthorpe Veterinary Group in February, you advised a dominance reduction programme and discussed Randolph's problems with the vet. He prescribed some of the Bach remedies which made a huge difference. We also had him castrated in April and now he actually sleeps during the day like a real dog.

He has calmed down enough to learn a vocabulary of about 20 phrases, but he is still a headstrong, wilful little bugger. Your 'Training Discs' have been most valued, but since I lost them at the weekend, I feel as though I have lost my left arm. Please send another set.

Thank you for your help, we weren't sure whether we would be able to keep him at first, but now Randolph is a lovable source of great fun. He'll never be an easy dog, but at least we still have him.

APPENDIX

INDOOR KENNELS

By nature and by instinct, dogs are denning animals. Most pet dogs create their own dens by sleeping in corners or under tables. It is a sensible idea, therefore, to supply them with a den of your choice which can be located in the area of your choice. Dogs will go into their makeshift dens to rest and, whilst in there, they feel secure and relaxed. If your dog has been allowed to create a den under your dining-room table or between two chairs in the lounge, and you decide to shut him in the kitchen at night or when you go out, then the chances are that he is not going to relax or sleep as easily.

We are all aware, when we buy a puppy, that we are going to go through certain problem periods like house-training and chewing which will stretch our patience and, if we handle it incorrectly, cause a certain amount of apprehension in the dog about our intentions. The last thing we want to do is to create mistrust in our relationship with our dog, especially at a time when the bonding period is at its strongest. But it is exactly at this time that the puppy can cause the greatest aggravation. Conditioning your puppy, or an older dog, to an indoor kennel with doors that can be shut, is the ideal answer for house-training, puppy chewing problems or destructive behaviour in older dogs.

An indoor kennel is basically a secure area about the same size as the dog's bed. It should be big enough for him to stretch out, stand up and turn round, and anything bigger is wasted space. A cubby-hole in the kitchen work units with some movable barrier to act as a door, or a quiet corner somewhere which, with a bit of imagination, can be converted, would be sufficient. Alternatively, most good pet shops sell, or can order for you, wire mesh travel/show cages. These have the advan-

tage of folding flat and have a handle so that they can be carried like a suitcase, as well as having a hinged door.

At the top end of the range is a purpose-built indoor kennel called the 'Wonderhome' available from Athag Ltd (UK), Carlyon Road, Atherstone Industrial Estate, Atherstone CV9 1LQ. It consists of a fibre-glass base which can be be used solely as a dog bed, and a cage with hinged doors which can quickly be attached to this base. My experience is that people who have owned dogs for years and who have now trained their current dog to accept the kennel arrangement wonder how they ever managed without one. With these comments in mind, buying a purpose-built, easily movable, easily adaptable kennel is a good long-term investment.

Training or conditioning a puppy to accept an indoor kennel is easy, especially if it is done from day one in the new home. If it is to be introduced at a later date, then the doors should not be shut until the puppy or older dog is comfortable inside it and chooses to use it of its own free will. Start by placing inside the familiar bedding, toys and water bowl. Feed the dog in there but without shutting him in. Once you notice that he chooses to lie in there at various times of the day, then the doors can be shut whilst you prepare his dinner and his food can be given to him inside the kennel, again with the doors shut. If he comes into the kitchen when you are preparing the family meal (if that is where the kennel is situated), shut him in, talk to him occasionally and, now and again poke a tit-bit through the mesh. Whenever you decide to give your dog a food reward, he must be inside his kennel with the doors shut to receive it. The whole idea is to teach him that having doors shut on him is a prelude to a pleasant experience — not that he is being locked up.

Access to other favourite sleeping areas should be denied during the introductory period — not by telling the dog off, but by creating barriers which will make it physically impossible for him to occupy them. You should also resist the temptation to demand that your dog should 'GET TO YOUR BED' whenever it has done something that does not please you, especially if it is more than two seconds after the act.

This sort of isolation punishment might work on a child but is totally confusing to dogs — they only obey because they are escaping from your obvious wrath, but this convinces us that they feel guilty and know that they have done wrong. They do not KNOW that they have done wrong but they do KNOW that you are cross for some strange reason. Constant repetition of punishment along these lines will teach your dog that the kennel is somewhere to go only when you are in a bad mood.

To a dog, a den is a safe haven; somewhere that is comfortable and which is easily defendable (on an instinctive level). The kennel should become the dog's den within the den site (your home). If you are using a cage-type arrangement, this feeling of security can be initially enhanced by placing a sheet over the top to suggest a solid roof and walls.

With most dogs this introductory period takes just a day or two; some dogs take four or five days, but rarely is it any longer. If pays dividends not to rush the training because the benefits that you derive from having a dog that is quite happy to be contained are enormous. The following are just a few examples.

House-training a puppy. No dog likes to soil its own nest and this is something that puppies learn at a very early stage. Accepting the fact that puppies defecate and urinate on a fairly frequent basis and therefore should not be left too long without access to a toilet area, they can be put into their kennel during unsupervised periods. From there, they can be taken to an area of the garden which you have set aside, allowed to perform their natural functions and rewarded with a tit-bit for doing so. The greater the reward the quicker the learning process, especially if they are ignored when they do it anywhere other than this 'target' area. Remember, though, that puppies have accidents just as human babies get dirty nappies. Punishment for normal puppy misdemeanours will create confusion and mistrust and might well prolong the house-training period through anxiety.

Chewing and destructive behaviour. When puppies are teething they chew and, except in rare cases, that's a fact of life. Some older dogs go through a second chewing period when the adult teeth are settling into the jaw bone — usually between the ages of six and nine months.

In both cases there is a physiological need to chew, and your table leg becomes a wonderful comforter in your absence. Leaving them in an indoor kennel, with some safe, acceptable item to satisfy this natural urge, not only protects your property but also your relationship with the dog. It is very hard to greet your dog with love and friendship when you come home to find that your kitchen has been demolished.

Protection of visitors and children. The old adage 'love me, love my dog' is basically a pretty selfish attitude. Some people genuinely do not like dogs, or worse, have a phobic fear of them. Some people develop allergic reactions when they touch a dog and some children, regardless of whether they love the dog or not, sometimes want to play games which do not include the dog. A dog which will happily settle down and relax in his indoor kennel is not constantly being told off for being too friendly to visitors or for trying to join in the children's games. This does not mean that he should be isolated whenever someone arrives — this might create a resentment — but on the odd occasion, putting him into his den with a nice juicy bone to chew helps to preserve friendships, both between you and your dog and between you and your visitors.

Bitches in season: muddy dogs with which you return home just as the phone rings; dogs recovering from operations; visits to hotels or other people's houses. The list is endless and all we need to do is to introduce it properly and then overcome our human emotion that a kennel is a prison and accept the dog's view that a kennel is a den and a safe haven.

SOUND AVERSION THERAPY

Over the years I have found sound aversion to be an effective means of interrupting unwanted behaviour without the need to use force in any way. Introduced and used properly, the dog blames himself for the unpleasant reaction and so stops doing whatever he was doing when the reaction occurred. The biggest plus from the owner's point of view is that, because the dog blames himself, the relationship between owner and dog is not affected.

In most cases, I use a method which I researched and developed in 1984–85 called 'Dog Training Discs'. These are simply a series of brass discs which create a particular noise. There is nothing special about the noise as such — it is not ultrasonic, nor is it pitched at a special level — it is just a sound that is unlike any other sound. If this sound can be introduced to coincide with a particular action, it will gradually condition the dog to avoid taking that action. The effectiveness of such a method depends entirely upon the introduction and if it is going to prove successful in the future, the dog's behaviour during the introduction should follow a predictable pattern.

I usually use tit-bits when introducing the 'Discs' and I do it in the following way. I have the dog contained in my office but off the leash. I sit on one side of the room with the owners on the other side. I call the dog over and give it three or four tit-bits with the words 'take it' with each one. Without saying anything to the dog, I then place a tit-bit on the floor by my feet, and as the dog goes to take it I throw the Discs alongside the food and immediately pick up the food and the Discs — at which point I start talking to the owners again and totally ignore the dog. I do not want to be involved with what has just happened, I take the view that it was the dog's fault. On the first occasion, most dogs continue to sniff on the floor for the food, apparently oblivious to the sudden sound and sudden arrival of the Discs.

About fifteen seconds later I repeat the same procedure. After four or five repetitions, as I place the food on the floor, the dog goes and lies down at its owner's feet on the other side of the room. It has reached what I call the 'AH HA' level: AH HA! if he gives me food I can have it, if he puts it on the floor, I can't. Basically, they learn that the action of going for the food creates the reaction, and by this time all that is needed is for the Discs to be shaken to achieve the same result.

This sound can then be used to coincide with and interrupt any unwanted behaviour and the reaction is always that the dog goes back to its owner. When it does, it is always praised, for the owner should always represent a safe haven to the dog. The Discs should never be used as an extension of anger, or as a missile — they are purely a reaction to an unwanted action, which has an unsettling effect on the dog so that it will need the security of the owner to reassure it.

Let us take a sample problem and look at how the Discs would be used to cure it — for example, the dog that charges at the letter-box and destroys all the letters and cheques that arrive, but somehow manages to leave all the bills untouched. Traditionally, postmen and dogs are sworn enemies — as are paperboys and milkmen. The reason for this is that these people invade the dog's territory on a daily basis, the dog barks ferociously and the invaders go away. Obviously, the dog has no idea that the intruders would have gone away whether it barked or not; as far as it is concerned, it has successfully defended the property. It only takes three or four repetitions for the dog to recognise the specific sounds and time of day when these people arrive, and for the whole scenario to become a self-rewarding experience. Visitors, however, are not predictable and they do not go away. Unfortunately, the post, paper and milk people do not have the time to stop and make friends with the dog; if they did, in most cases the problem would not arise.

However, back to the problem of what to do about it. Simply arrange for someone to come to the house at a specific time and rattle the letter-box. As the dog charges towards the door, throw the Discs at the door (provided it is not made of glass) just as the dog arrives; do not say a word. The reason we do not post anything at this stage is that we do not want the dog's attention to be diverted away from what is happening. Ten minutes later, repeat the exercise, again with no letters arriving. On the third occasion, a letter can be posted, but I doubt whether the dog will see it because he won't be near the door. Make sure that on the following morning you are up in time to be there when the real post arrives, because the dog will know the tone of the post van's engine and the circumstances will be slightly different from your training exercise.

A small percentage of dogs do not respond to the Discs. With these dogs I use a screech alarm, similar to the type that can be bought for personal protection. They consist of a hand-held gas-filled canister with a whistle on the top. By depressing the top, a short burst of gas is released which blows the whistle. Care should be taken in introducing it that you do not get it too close to the dog's ears, nor should it be used near other animals as it can tend to frighten some of them. Its use is limited to pure aversion, whereas with the Discs, once the problem has been overcome, they can be used to teach a whole variety of other things. Nevertheless, the screech alarm is a useful sound aversion back-up piece of equipment which uses the same principle — unwanted actions create unpleasant reactions.

For further details send S.A.E to: Dog Training Discs, Greengarth, Maddox Lane, Bookham, Surrey KT23 3HT.

OTHER AVERSION METHODS

The basic idea of aversion is to make what the dog is doing unpleasant. I am totally opposed to electric shock therapy except where the only alternative is that the dog will have to be put down and all other methods have been tried first. Even then, it should be carried out by someone who knows how to use it, knows how to read the dog's reaction to it and has insisted that the dog should have a full medical check beforehand. It is a method which is widely misused in the United States, Germany and many other countries. Sadly, dog clubs in this country are being sent details from a company that is importing shock collars, and I fear that they will get into the wrong hands and be misused by people who will see this therapy as the ultimate in long-distance punishment. I hasten to add that I do not possess or use a shock collar.

Where aversion therapy is called for, I rely on techniques that do not cause pain and, wherever possible, do not appear to originate from the owner. Where sound aversion is not possible because it requires the presence of the owner or a third party, I use booby-trap techniques or taste aversion therapy.

Assume that your dog is an avid kitchen swing bin raider — a problem that is extremely difficult to overcome because it is so self-rewarding. We can of course lock the bin away when we are not there, but this is hardly teaching the dog anything. One day we shall forget and the dog will strike.

From most joke shops you can buy some harmless little explosive caps which come with a spring-loaded detonator. Once the cap is in position it is held there by the weight of whatever you are booby-trapping — in this case the lid of the swing bin. As soon as the pressure is relieved, the cap is exploded. If the bin has been filled up with paper and a tissue that has been soaked in gravy placed on top, your dog is going to think that there are some wonderful edible treasures in there.

As soon as he pokes his head in, he is going to get a very loud shock. If he plucks up the courage to try again, he will not be rewarded. Two or three engineered repetitions will break the habit forever, as it will with any bad habit that this method can be employed upon.

Taste aversion would be used, for instance, where the dog's chewing is dangerous or extremely expensive (bearing in mind that chewing is a curable behaviour problem). The chewing of electric cables is one problem that instantly springs to mind, where this type of aversion would be called for. I use a particularly obnoxious substance called 'Bitter Apple'. It can be used for stopping dogs chewing bandages or licking wounds but is particularly effective for stopping them chewing anything, if the introduction is done in the right way.

First of all you need to obtain a cheap perfume which should be diluted quite considerably and then put into a spray bottle. Then you need a bottle of Bitter Apple and a tissue. Soak the tissue in Bitter Apple and put it on the floor. A few inches in front of this tissue, spray the floor with the diluted perfume and call your dog over. As it arrives at the tissue, its highly developed olfactory system will have registered the smell of the perfume. Pop the tissue into its mouth and hold it shut for a few seconds before allowing the dog to spit it out — which it surely will. Your dog will then sneeze, salivate, spit, rub its nose on the carpet, do anything to get rid of the awful taste.

The Bitter Apple can then be sprayed upon any surface that you want to protect (except polished surfaces). A few inches in front of what you are trying to protect, your diluted perfume can be sprayed. Your dog will approach, register the smell of the perfume and remember the taste to which this was a prelude. The perfume can then be used as a trigger warning to stay away from anything you do not want the dog to touch, even if it is not protected by the taste deterrent. Eventually, the smell of the diluted perfume will disappear as far as we are concerned, but the dog will detect it for a long, long time.

Last, but not least, we have water. Again working on the principle that actions create reactions, a timely squirt of water from a well-washed-out washing-up liquid bottle can have a devastating effect on some dogs. A lot of people make the comment that it will not work with their dog because he loves water, but a short sharp squirt on the nose is entirely different from the whoopee fun of running in and out of a sprinkler, or drinking from the hosepipe.

As in all forms of aversion therapy, the introduction is all-important, as is the fact that it should never be used as a threat or an extension of anger. 'Actions create reactions' should be the guiding phrase throughout the application of any form of aversion.

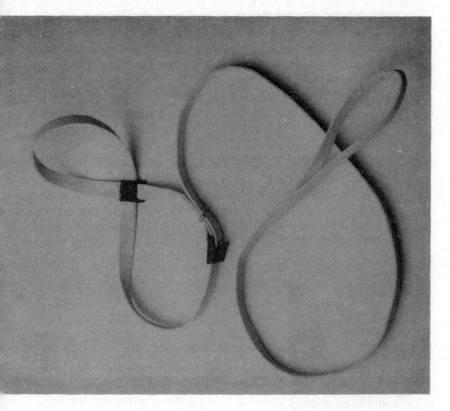

THE COL-LEASH

The Col-leash, as the name suggests, is a combined collar and leash. It is the end-result of almost two years of research by my wife Liz and myself to design an effective means of stopping a dog from pulling without choking it or applying extra pressure across the bridge of the nose. It is based on the headcollar design and an age-old training principle that the higher up on the neck the collar fits, the less resistance is encountered. Having been tried and tested on many different breeds of dogs, the Col-leash uses this basic principle: the best way to lead any animal is to use the point of least resistance. The Col-leash is held in place by the noseband and the dog is led from a point just below the ear. The major breakthrough in the design is the use of a locking clip which ensures that, once fitted, no uncomfortable pressure can be applied to the throat or any part of the head. From the dog's point of view, it means that there is no pressure to resist. The result: calmer, easier-to-control dogs.

Fitting a Col-leash to your new puppy, instead of the traditional collar and lead as its first controlling influence, means that it will never learn to pull. This means that you will not have to correct a problem later (the biggest complaint from pet owners who join an obedience club is that their dog pulls on the lead). Because the Col-leash is fully adjustable it will grow with your puppy, and therefore there will be no need to keep updating the equipment.

The Col-leash is available from Think Dog Products, Crow Hall Farm, Northfield Road, Soham, Nr. Ely, Cambs. (Tel: 0353 720431; Fax: 0353 624202).

APBC
ASSOCIATION OF PET
BEHAVIOUR COUNSELLORS

ASSOCIATION OF PET BEHAVIOUR COUNSELLORS

In Chapter 1 I mentioned the formation of this Association, and I am proud to call myself one of the founding members. My practice has since expanded considerably and, with the help of my associates, we can now offer a referral service to vets in London and the southern counties.

Much of what I have written about in this book can be applied by the owners of problem dogs without recourse to further advice. However, some of the problems, especially those that involve aggression, need a carefully structured programme of rehabilitation. If you are in any doubt about how to overcome your problem, in the first instance you should contact your veterinary surgeon with a view to being referred to a member practice of the APBC.

The strength of the APBC lies in the variety of backgrounds from which its members come. Veterinary medicine, psychology and clinical psychology, biology, zoology, ethology — as well as some of the leading experts in the field of training who between them have many years' experience in police dog, guide dog, hearing dog and pet dog training. The Association also enjoys the membership of some of the foremost behaviourists from overseas and is backed up with a team of scientific and veterinary advisers. With this enormous pool of knowledge available to every member for the cost of a phone call, they can offer the veterinary profession a referral service of the highest possible standard for the benefit of the pet-owning public. If one of them doesn't know the answer, they all know someone who does, and between member practices this knowledge is freely available.

For details of clinics in your area you should consult your veterinary surgeon or write to The Hon Secretary, Association of Pet Behaviour Counsellors, 157 Royal College Street, London NW1 9LU.

EPILOGUE

Whilst writing this book, Oliver — our Weimaraner pictured on the jacket with my other dogs — sadly died. I have much to thank him for, not least that it was he who brought my wife Liz and myself together through training for working trials competition. I could write some moving, sentimental words about how much we miss him, but he wasn't the type of dog that would go in for all that sloppy stuff. Of course we miss him, but we would prefer to remember him for his achievements rather than dwelling on the sadness of his passing away.

Oliver took to the sport of working trials like a duck takes to water and, with Liz handling him, he became the Working Weimaraner of the Year 1982 and competed at the highest levels of working trials — but his greatest achievement was as a teacher.

Observing Oliver's behaviour within our multi-breed pack of dogs taught me that there is no such thing as breeds of dog, they are all just dogs. For sure, Yoko (our Japanese Akita) was originally bred as a hunter of wild boar and even bears, as well as being a renowned fighting dog; Inch (our Border Collie) was bred to herd; Chip (our Jack Russell) was bred for its ability to keep up with the fox-hunting horses and hounds but to have the courage to face its quarry underground; and of course, Oliver was originally bred to hunt wolves, bears and boars but later was adapted for the tracking and retrieving of game birds. But, instincts aside, within the domestic environment they all followed the same canine code of conduct.

Watching them throughout the greater part of the day, it would be difficult to work out the rank structure between them. Watching them first thing in the morning it became clear which one was the top dog; without doubt it was Oliver. How he did it just goes to show how easily what we see and think is happening can be easily misinterpreted.

For a long time, both Liz and I were of the opinion that Oliver was a particularly lazy dog in the morning. Whilst the other three were alert and active, Oliver would stay on his bed — sometimes until quite late in the morning. We also assumed that he was quite grumpy with the other dogs if they tried to disturb him, growling quietly when they approached him. Then we realised that there was another reason for this lazy, grumpy attitude. On a daily basis, dogs will establish their rank structure — it may be simply that when first meeting, one will hold his head high and the other will display a low head carriage. This often happens so quickly that we mere humans don't even notice. In Oliver's case, he would wait for each dog to approach him in turn and, without moving, would issue a low growl. The approaching dog would turn its head slightly, lick its lips and slink away. I tested this theory one morning by withholding one of the dogs. At ten-thirty, Oliver was still on his bed. Feeling sorry for him, I let the dog in to greet him. Oliver gave a quick growl and, as soon as the dog was turning away, he shot off his bed and out into the garden for what was obviously a much-needed pee, judging by the look of relief on his face.

What I learned from this is that whenever dogs behave in a particular way on a regular basis, there is a meaning behind it. I also learned the importance of trying to understand what that meaning is. Before we understood what Oliver was doing, we often told him off for growling at the other dogs — in effect, he was displaying his rank in a canine way and we were denying him that right by reprimanding him. The other dogs understood him, it was we who did not.

It was Oliver who always greeted us at the door with something in his mouth; naturally this insured that we greeted him first, consistent with his higher status. Now that he has gone, Yoko has taken over the top dog slot. She is now the one to greet us with something in her mouth and is afforded the same privilege. On a daily basis she waits until the other two have gone into the kitchen and then she lies in the doorway.

There is no growling, no eye contact, no body postures, just her presence stops the others from going into the next room, and this can last for five minutes or so. She moves out of the way if we approach, but resumes her position immediately; the other two just sit and wait for the ritual to be completed. We don't interfere, it's what dogs do — regardless of breed.

I've learnt a lot from the dogs I have owned in the past. Sabre, my first German Shepherd, taught me how not to train a dog, and I shall never forget him for allowing me to make all my mistakes on him. My all-time favourite, the big, soft-hearted, long-coated German Shepherd, Gill (pronounced with a hard G not a J), took me to the very top in competition and taught me that, although we may carry home the trophy, it is the dog that has done the work. But the most important lessons that Liz and I learned about the behaviour of dogs in the home we received from a very fine teacher, who probably thought he had some pretty dumb students. If there are any last words to say to him, they have to be:

THANKS, OLLIE.

INDEX

Numbers in bold are main headings